Changing Images of Early Childhood
Series Editor: Nicola Yelland

Playing it Straight

Uncovering Gender Discourses
in the Early Childhood Classroom

MINDY BLAISE

Routledge
Taylor & Francis Group
New York   London

Published in 2005 by
Routledge
Taylor & Francis Group
270 Madison Avenue
New York, NY 10016

Published in Great Britain by
Routledge
Taylor & Francis Group
2 Park Square
Milton Park, Abingdon
Oxon OX14 4RN

© 2005 by Taylor & Francis Group, LLC
Routledge is an imprint of Taylor & Francis Group

Printed in the United States of America on acid-free paper
10 9 8 7 6 5 4 3 2 1

International Standard Book Number-10: 0-415-95113-5 (Hardcover) 0-415-95114-3 (Softcover)
International Standard Book Number-13: 978-0-415-95113-5 (Hardcover) 978-0-415-95114-2 (Softcover)
Library of Congress Card Number 2005006115

Library of Congress Cataloging-in-Publication Data

Blaise, Mindy.
   Playing it straight : uncovering gender discourses in the early childhood classroom / Mindy Blaise.
      p. cm.
   Includes bibliographical references and index.
   ISBN 0-415-95113-5 (hb : alk. paper) -- ISBN 0-415-95114-3 (pb : alk. paper)
   1. Sex differences in education--United States. 2. Early childhood education--United States. 3. Gender identity--United States. 4. Poststructuralism--United States. I. Title.

   LC212.93.U6B53 2005
   372.21--dc22   2005006115

Taylor & Francis Group
is the Academic Division of T&F Informa plc.

Visit the Taylor & Francis Web site at
http://www.taylorandfrancis.com

and the Routledge Web site at
http://www.routledge-ny.com

CONTENTS

Series Editor's Introduction

Early childhood education has long been organized around and justified by the principles of developmentally appropriate practice (DAP), which are founded in the developmental psychology literature from the early twentieth century. The theories of learning and socialization in this literature were conceptualized in social and economic contexts vastly different from those of the present day, yet education often seems to be caught in a time warp; justifications for outdated practices and attitudes need to be challenged. DAP privileged certain ways of being and knowing that did not recognize the diverse qualities of children and their families in a global context. In doing so, it had the effect of alienating the qualities of diversity that should be celebrated, and it further suggested that there was a universal state that we should all be striving for, which was based on Western ways of doing and knowing. In recent times, these contentions have been challenged, and early childhood education is coming to be known for its openness to new ideas; the multidisciplinary nature of the field has facilitated the process of reconceptualization. The terrain of early childhood has been remodeled significantly over the past decade, and alternative views and perspectives are beginning to have an impact on practices and pedagogies.

The changing images of early childhood are reflected in the books that constitute this series, since they challenge and confront educators with a wide range of topics. The books will enable early childhood professionals to engage with contemporary ideas and practices from perspectives other than those that traditionally have been associated with the education of young children and their families. They will provide opportunities to critique aspects of the field that many early childhood educators have accepted as being beyond question, as well as act as catalysts for contemporary interrogations and investigations. The ideas contained in the books will incorporate a wide range of theoretical perspectives that are particularly appropriate to life in the postmodern world. Additionally, issues that have been taboo (e.g., sexuality) or viewed from only one perspective (e.g., moral development) will be presented. In this way the multidisciplinary perspective of the field becomes evident. Today, instead of being influenced solely by the psychological perspective, early childhood education benefits from the ideas that have emerged from other disciplines such as anthropology, cultural studies, sociology, and philosophy. This has enriched the capacity of early childhood educators to respond to the new demands of contemporary times with pedagogies and practices that are appropriate to the varying and changing needs and interests of young children and their families. The books in this series will help early childhood education students and professionals to engage in such dialogues from an informed base. They consider alternative theoretical perspectives and demonstrate the relevance of these perspectives to everyday practices; in so doing, they enable us to create learning environments underpinned by respect for all, equity, and social justice.

In *Playing It Straight*, Mindy Blaise considers the important issues around gender in the early childhood years and provides the reader with strong and articulate arguments regarding the reasons that assumptions about gender need to be confronted and questioned in a critical manner. She starts by informing us about how gender has been socially constructed, and she describes the traditional ways in which we have viewed gender as being synonymous with biological sex differences, which has encouraged societal expectations for boys and girls that limit their potential and restrict the range of opportunities available to them. Blaise discusses the notions of hegemonic masculinity and emphasized femininity, which regulate behavior and frame the ways teachers interact with children in early childhood settings. She presents alternative ways of dealing with gendered issues and behaviors during play that require us to take risks in our practices and challenge our assumptions in our daily work with young children. Employing feminist poststructuralism and queer theory, she uncovers the heterosexual matrix and encourages us to rethink the ways in which we might be able to change our practices so that we are able to create contexts for learning and living that are based on the principles of social justice and equity. Blaise spent a year in a classroom talking, researching, and working with the children and their teacher to collect rich data that inform us about the ways in which gender is enacted in our everyday lives. Her descriptions are linked to the theoretical perspectives provided by feminist poststructuralism and queer theory, and her case studies of three children in the class vividly illustrate what is as well as what can be when we take risks and challenge the status quo. This is brave work, and Blaise provides readers with the resources to utilize new pedagogies that suit the needs of young children, their families, and society as we move forward in the twenty-first century, in which our lives are very different from and more complex than those of previous times.

Nicola Yelland,
Victoria University, Melbourne

ACKNOWLEDGMENTS

I would like to begin by acknowledging the work of Adrienne Rich and Monique Wittig, both feminist writers, whose scholarship provoked me to rethink gender within the field of early childhood education. By realizing how compulsory heterosexuality informed and restricted my choices as a woman, I also began to see how these ideas were relevant for rethinking early childhood teaching and researching.

Although my work as a feminist researcher is relatively new, it would not have been possible without Isabel Beaton's personal and professional generosity. Not only was Isabel generous with her time, but she also shared her ideas and thoughts about teaching, researching, and gender, and they have influenced how I view these worlds. The classroom community that she created supported my work as a feminist researcher, and I continuously draw upon these experiences to inform my practice as an early childhood teacher educator and researcher. I would also like to give special thanks to the children in this classroom, especially Alan, Penny, and Madison, who pushed gender boundaries and taught me about the complexities and politics of "doing" gender in the kindergarten classroom. Both Isabel and the children supported me in their classroom community as I stumbled along on this research journey.

I would like to recognize the encouragement that I had from family, friends, and colleagues. Sharon Ryan and Gloria Latham had reassuring words that seemed to always come at just the right time. Additionally,

Catherine Bernard and Nicola Yelland's insight and support were helpful during the editing process.

I also appreciated the many preservice early childhood and elementary teachers and graduate students in both the United States and Australia who have listened to these stories about gender, researching, and teaching. Their questions and comments kept me revisiting the data and rethinking teaching and researching in the early childhood classroom.

Finally, this book would not be what it is without the support of my partner, Yarrow. Not only did he read every vulnerable, fragile new paragraph, but there were countless times that he got me unstuck. I appreciate his ways of seeing the gendered world that we both share, and I value his commitment to early childhood, gender, and equity. Thank you for being such a significant part of my personal and professional lives — you have enriched them both.

1

FEMINIST POSTSTRUCTURALISM AND QUEER THEORY: WHAT DO THEY OFFER?

It's Thursday morning, and I have just arrived in Isabel's kindergarten classroom. It is center time, a part of the day when children can freely choose a learning center to play at with friends. The room is buzzing with talk and activity. I am barely noticed until Penny catches my eye as she looks up from her seat at the writing center; she gives me a quick smile and wave. Isabel is near the wet-sand table, and I quietly say "hi," letting her know that I'm here, but I'm also conscious of her need to be focusing on the children in her care, rather than me, the researcher. Before getting settled, I quickly look in my folder, which Isabel kindly made for me and uses to communicate with me about research issues, often placing into it children's drawings, writings, or other pieces of work that she thinks will interest me. Today I discover a small scrap of paper on which Isabel has scribbled, "Ask me about Raoul's birthday party!" I find an empty table to sit at, and take my field notebook and tape recorder out of my backpack.

Trying to gain a quick sense of what is going on in the classroom, I notice Anne, Sophie, Alan, and Raoul playing together in the dramatic play center. Sophie and Anne are at the stove, cooking and talking on the phone. Raoul and Alan are standing on top of the large wooden blocks and ramps; they have sunglasses pulled over their eyes and scarves wrapped around their necks, resembling neckties. I see and hear the following:

Raoul: Where are you going today?

Alan: I'm going to kill some people. I'm a villain.

Raoul: (Uses a plastic banana as a gun and starts shooting at Alan) Bang, pow, pow, pow! I got you!

Alan: Hey, Raoul . . . my name is Bond . . . James Bond (lowering his head toward the floor while looking up with his eyes).

Sophie: *Guys, g:u:y:s* . . . We need a table. (Using a high-pitched and singsong voice. She is standing with her feet apart and with both hands on her hips.)

Alan: We can make it later.

Sophie: (Talking into the phone) No, we are eating right now. (Turns to Anne) He's asleep. Someone shot him.

Anne: He said, "I'm afraid." He has pain. We need to check if the bullet is in his heart.

This sort of play is common in early childhood classrooms, and if you had asked me about this play scenario ten years ago, when I was a kindergarten teacher, I would have used my knowledge of child development to assess where each child was at socially, emotionally, cognitively, and physically through their play. I believed that it was my responsibility as the classroom teacher to know where each child in my care was at developmentally and then to construct a developmentally appropriate curriculum based on these observations. I never questioned this approach to teaching because the National Association for the Education of Young Children (NAEYC) promoted developmentally appropriate practices (DAP) in the popular publication *Developmentally Appropriate Practice in Early Childhood Programs* (Bredekamp

& Copple, 1997). As Katz (1996) and Stott and Bowman (1996) claim, it provided me with a sense of confidence as an early childhood teacher. These traditional ways of observing positioned me as the knowledgeable teacher, enabling me to put together a clear and coherent picture of children's learning (Campbell & Smith, 2001). I believed this was the "right" (and only) way to teach, and I felt sure about my practices. I never questioned what I knew or what I did in the classroom. I was unable to see how these guidelines are premised on modernist assumptions of universality, objectivity, independence, and autonomy (Lubeck, 1996). The dualistic nature of appropriate and inappropriate practices (or good and bad teaching) made it difficult to conceive of other possibilities for understanding teaching, learning, and young children.

However, I am no longer certain that relying on child development to inform practice is best for children. My beliefs about what it means to be an early childhood teacher have also shifted from a desire to meet each child's unique and individual needs to attending to larger issues of fairness and social justice. This book is about reconceptualizing early childhood teaching by moving away from child development and toward exploring what I call "postdevelopmentalism," alternative theoretical frameworks that can assist us to make sense of teaching, learning, and young children in new ways. *Postdevelopmentalism* is a broad term used to define alternative theoretical perspectives that question modernist assumptions of truth, universality, and certainty. In particular, I use feminist poststructuralism and queer theory to focus on how young children are "playing it straight" while actively doing gender in their kindergarten classroom. These new perspectives support pedagogies that aim to explore assumptions about identities, diversity, and learning. This in turn sustains a teaching agenda that centers on equity and social justice, rather than just an individual child's developmental progress.

Rather than relying exclusively on biological and socialization theories of gender construction to make sense of children's gender, this book attempts to break down theoretical barriers with new understandings of how gender is socially and politically constructed by young children. Aimed at conceptualizing how gender norms influence young children's identities, the gendered social order of their kindergarten classroom, and early childhood teaching, this book examines gender, an issue that DAP ignores. More specifically, this book discusses how discourses of heterosexuality operate and how children actively use their understandings of these discourses to regulate gender in their classroom. In other words, this is a book about how young children make sense of the politics of femininities and masculinities, and about the complex ways they are doing gender in their everyday lives.

This chapter begins by questioning the relevance of developmental psychology and the role it plays in masking gender and gender equity in the early childhood classroom. In order to understand how gender is frequently understood, existing and common theories about gender differences are examined, along with what they mean for early childhood practice. Then feminist poststructuralism and queer theory are explored, highlighting how they bring about new ways of understanding children's gendered identities and early childhood teaching.

Feminist poststructuralism and the possible ways that it can be used to pull apart and make sense of children's talk and actions will be discussed. A feminist poststructuralist approach uses principles of poststructuralism and aspects of feminism in an attempt to understand the causes of gender inequity (Weedon, 1997). Poststructuralist concepts such as language, discourse, subjectivity, agency, and power will be defined, and examples from the early childhood classroom are used to demonstrate how a feminist poststructuralist approach interprets classroom life. Then these concepts are used to show how feminist poststructuralism theorizes the social construction of gender in the classroom. Next, aspects of queer theory are explored, adding another layer to the complexities of the social and political construction of gender while deepening and broadening our understandings of how heterosexual discourses are used by young children to constitute themselves as gendered. With this new set of theoretical tools, teachers can begin seeing the familiar in new ways. Uncovering gender discourses in the classroom and the ways in which children's understandings of gender norms play out in their daily lives challenges the field of early childhood education to see the complex ways that children are actively doing gender.

Child Development: What Does It Do for Teachers and Children?

How might a teacher using traditional developmental observations understand Raoul, Alan, Sophie, and Anne's play? Most likely, these teachers would focus their gaze on a child's development across four main categories: cognitive, language, social/emotional, and physical abilities (Almy & Genishi, 1979; Bredekamp & Copple, 1997). Then each child's development would be assessed within broad social and cultural norms to determine where he or she is at, allowing the teacher to use this information to plan a program based on each child's individual developmental needs.

A teacher might also choose to interpret this play by using Parten's Play Scale (1932) to determine if the children are participating in solitary, parallel, associative, or cooperative play. This view assumes that all children are taking part in some stage of play, with the teacher determining where each child is located on the play scale. The scale situates different forms of play, beginning with the most immature (solitary play) and progressing toward the more mature (cooperative play). Consequently, cooperative play is considered the most important and valued form of play. Using her knowledge of how children progress and develop, this teacher would conclude that all of the children in the play scenario are involved in some form of associative play, as Raoul and Alan are engaging in separate play activities when compared to Sophie and Anne. Also, the children are noticing each other's behavior, as when Sophie requests that the boys make her a table. According to this framework, interactive play is common and "normal" for this age group. Taking this into consideration, a teacher might assume that the children's play will naturally develop into the next and more complex stage of cooperative play. A teacher then would use these observations of children's play to plan the curriculum. For example, she might consider providing more play opportunities for each child, ensuring that sociodramatic play occurs. As an advanced form of cooperative play, sociodramatic play is believed to facilitate both cognitive and social development (Howes, 1992). Promoting and supporting sociodramatic play is one example of DAP and is valued in early childhood education

However, what might happen if teachers began questioning this framework and its relevance for children's lives and experiences? What if a teacher began to ask the following:

- Does my knowledge of child development "make" a child take part in more advanced forms of play?
- Wouldn't children just do this anyway?
- Does it really matter if I understand child development and how children usually develop socially, emotionally, physically, and intellectually?

If teachers begin asking such questions (and they are), they might reconsider the role that child development has in their practice. It is possible that they might realize how DAP privileges certain forms of knowledge while masking other areas. When I look at how Parten's Play Scale is used to inform practice in the classroom, I notice that it ignores the knowledge that children are creating together about what it means to be a girl or a boy. Instead of attending to gender (and other social issues such as race, class, and sexuality), this framework ignores it. Not only are the politics of gender untouched, but this play scale is unable to conceptualize power and how it is created and used in the classroom. If theories are not concerned with social issues, such as gender, race, class, and sexuality, and how they influence children's identities, how can teachers bring about social change and improve the lives of all children? How will teachers find out about children's identities and what it means to be an Asian American working-class girl or an Anglo-American middle-class boy? It is necessary to question why child development is the dominant discourse in early childhood education when it fails to address social issues, such as gender equity in teaching.

Over the past decade, an emerging group of early childhood scholars labeling themselves "reconceptualists" have been asking similar questions regarding the field of early childhood's dependence on developmental, structural, and biologically based theories of child development. They argue that the scientific knowledge base of child development, which views children as autonomous, rational, and self-determining individuals, is biased both culturally and in terms of gender, and they advocate for the use of new theoretical frameworks to inform research and teaching in early childhood (Grieshaber & Cannella, 2001; Hauser & Jipson, 1997; Kessler & Swadener, 1992; Mallory & New, 1994; Silin, 1995; Tobin, 1995, 1997; Yelland, 1998, 2005). This work highlights the ways in which developmental perspectives distance teachers from children, reinforcing teachers' beliefs that they "know" the children in their care both scientifically and objectively, enabling them to further children's cognitive, language, social/emotional, and physical growth in appropriate ways. Developmental perspectives also foster the belief that this knowledge base provides teachers with certainty and the sense that they are able to create a curriculum based on each child's unique developmental needs.

Child development influences how teachers see children in the classroom. Moreover, relying exclusively on this knowledge base to inform practice means that the issues around social justice are not seen as an integral part of "good" early childhood practice. If teachers are unable to see these issues in such a light, then why or how would they begin the work of addressing them? Furthermore, until gender is recognized as a fundamental category, constituting individuals and social relationships, then it too remains on the margins, rather than at the center of practice. And by ignoring gender, the field of early childhood education fails to recognize how children's identities are constructed and reconstructed, and how their gendered, racialized, classed, and sexualized identities play a significant role in social justice. If the dominant discourse of DAP does not provide a means for addressing social justice, and in particular gender equity, why would teachers begin addressing gender in their classrooms? Put more simply, if the field of early childhood education does not believe that gender is an issue, then why would teachers begin to address it in practice?

Browne (2004) strengthens this argument by showing how the notion of the "naturally developing" child, which is constructed throughout DAP, has implications for gender equity in two major ways. First, this construction conceals the ways in which gender influences a child's experiences and how these life experiences are interpreted. Second, DAP fails to consider the various ways that children's gender and experiences with gender influence learning and development.

Before issues around gender equity can be addressed, teachers must first notice and locate gender in the classroom. Two common ways for understanding gender and gender differences are through biological and sociological frameworks. The next section will discuss these two theoretical perspectives and how a teacher might see children "doing" gender in the classroom when using these gender lenses.

Biological and Socialization Theories of Gender

How children construct themselves as girls and boys is usually defined through biological and socialization theories of gender construction. The general causes of gender inequality are often seen as a debate between nature and nurture (Measor & Sikes, 1992). This dispute is over the extent to which gender differences are caused by either biology (nature) or culture (nurture). The conservative perspective believes that gender differences and inequalities originate from biological differences, which are seen as inevitable, unchangeable, and a part of the natural order. In other words, men and women are not equal because they are born different. This viewpoint draws on scientific evidence to support the belief that not only do chromosomes determine one's sex, but they also influence the kind of hormones produced in our bodies, which form our sexual characteristics and determine our physical growth (Lindsey, 1990). This type of information concerning the chromosomal basis of the sexes is considered a fact and is widely accepted and rarely questioned.

While we cannot dismiss the fact that biology does influence one's sex, it becomes more difficult to establish the extent to which gender differences are biological in origin. Critiques of the genetic argument focus on the weaknesses of the experimental data, such as the cultural variations and socialization outcomes, and on the narrow definition of human identity (Fausto-Sterling, 1992). For example, biological determinism relies on experimental data from work done on animals, rather than humans. Teachers work with real children in the social, cultural, and political context of classrooms, not with rats or monkeys in a laboratory.

Second, the genetic argument does not account for the variation of human culture and society. Oakley (1972) asserts that if distinctions between males and females were biologically rooted, there would be one universal form for each sex rather than the variations we find in the sexes within and between different cultures and societies. Teachers regularly see a range of ways that children embody and perform gender in the classroom. Is there ever just one simple form of femininity performed in the classroom? Some girls are considered "tomboys" because they do not seem to care about getting messy or they play primarily with boys, while others are thought of as "girly girls" because they like playing with dolls and wear frilly skirts and dresses to school or colorful ribbons in their hair.

A third criticism of biological determinism is that it does not justify the effects that socialization has upon the two sexes. For instance, how do we make sense of the girls who do play "just like their mothers," cooking and cleaning in the dramatic play center, and yet one girl's mother works outside the home and her father is the primary caregiver?

Finally, not only does this theory of gender construction insist that human identity is fixed and unchanging, but it also fails to account for the rapid pace of social change in society (Lindsey, 1990; Measor & Sikes, 1992). What it means to be female in 2005 is not the same as it was during the 1950s. In contemporary Western society, it is common for women to have full-time employment outside the home, and some children are being cared for by men either at home or in childcare settings.

In contrast to the biological view of gender construction, socialization theories focus on the process by which individuals learn to be members of their society (Berger, 1976). Socialization theories view gender identity as a product of various forms of learning. This theory, put forth by Mischel (1966), Bandura and Walters (1963), Lynn (1969), and others, emphasizes the importance the environment has for a child's gender development. According to this theory, the child learns her or his role directly through modeling and reinforcement, and recognizes the importance that society and culture place on the different expectations for both females and males (Basow, 1986; Measor & Sikes, 1992).

Since children learn new behaviors by imitating both adults and other children (Bandura, 1977), social learning theorists therefore emphasize the importance of imitation and modeling. Assuming that sex typing begins at birth, social learning theory views same-sex modeling as preceding and giving rise to the formation of a stable gender identity. As a result, children begin imitating people, both adults and peers, whom they see as being like them, shaping their behavior in accordance with either a masculine or feminine role (Basow, 1986).

In the early childhood classroom, children are often rewarded, either implicitly or explicitly, for sex-appropriate behaviors and discouraged or punished for inappropriate ones. For example, if Raoul is punished for clinging to or crying for his mother when he is dropped off at school and then rewarded for working on his own at the sand table, he is more likely to develop autonomous and independent behaviors than his female classmate who receives the opposite reinforcement. What if the adults in the classroom often praise girls, such as Anne, for sitting quietly and looking pretty, while Raoul and Alan are allowed to be noisy, active, and curious? What messages are all the children in the classroom receiving about how to be a boy or girl? Or, in the case of the play scenario described on page, what if the teacher notices Sophie and Anne's domestic play and then reinforces it by casually praising them for taking care of the family and showing care and concern for the gunshot victim? According to socialization theories, the teacher's actions are problematic because they are reinforcing the idea that boys and girls have dissimilar interests and are in fact different. That is, girls are expected to (and do) show compliance and nurturing behaviors, and boys are not (and do not).

Both biological and socialization perspectives provide simple explanations about children's gender that seem both logical and obvious, and as Browne (2004) explains, as scientific discourses, they are easy to accept. When teachers regularly see these examples play out in their classrooms, it is hard *not* to conceptualize gender in these two simple ways. Revisiting Raoul, Alan, Anne, and Sophie's play allows us to see how biological and socialization perspectives are easily—and, some might argue, simplistically—used to make sense of children's talk and actions.

Raoul: Where are you going today?

Alan: I'm going to kill some people. I'm a villain.

Raoul:	(Uses a plastic banana as a gun and starts shooting at Alan) Bang, pow, pow, pow! I got you!
Alan:	Hey, Raoul . . . my name is Bond . . . James Bond (lowering head and looking up with his eyes).
Sophie:	*Guys, g:u:y:s* . . . We need a table. (Using a high-pitched and singsong voice. She is standing with her feet apart and her hands on her hips.)
Alan:	We can make it later.
Sophie:	(Talking into the phone) No, we are eating right now. (Turns to Anne) He's asleep. Someone shot him.
Anne:	He said, "I'm afraid." He has pain. We need to check if the bullet is in his heart.

"They're Just Born That Way"

An early childhood teacher drawing from biological perspectives of gender might interpret the children's play as *natural*. That is, Anne and Sophie enact caring and nurturing roles in their play because they are born with these feminine characteristics, just as Raoul and Alan's desire to take part in violent and action-oriented story lines seems *logical* because that is how their brains are genetically "programmed." A teacher working from this framework might react to this play by throwing her arms up in frustration and telling herself, "Oh, well. Boys will be boys!" These scientific explanations of gender imply that it is *normal* for boys and girls to play in *different* ways. Some teachers may find this way of thinking troubling, because if children are born this way, then what can they do in their practice to make a difference? This way of seeing children illuminates the inconsistency of teachers' actions. For instance, why do teachers often discipline rowdy boys and at the same time justify these behaviors as normal?

"They're Just Doing What They See"

A teacher working from a socialization perspective might reason that these children are *modeling* and *imitating* behaviors they have seen at home or in school, read in books, or watched on television. For example, Sophie and Anne choose to play in the kitchen area because they often see their mothers cooking in the kitchen at home. They take on caring and nurturing female roles in their play because this type of behavior is modeled and reinforced by their friends as appropriate and normal for girls. Similarly, Raoul and Alan are interested in aggressive play because this is what they see male characters doing in the cartoons they watch and the stories they read.

What makes socialization theories of gender powerful is how the teacher is thought of as being able to make a difference by intervening in children's sexist and biased behaviors. For example, if a teacher was interested in changing Alan and Raoul's aggressive play behaviors, she would make certain that the curriculum included opportunities for the boys to see men performing caring and nurturing tasks. This might be done by reading stories about fathers who do most of the child rearing, putting up posters of men taking on nurturing roles, or inviting male nurses to come and talk with the class about their jobs. A teacher working from this framework would also try reinforcing behaviors that challenge gender stereotypes. For example, if Raoul was observed taking care of a baby at the dramatic play center, the teacher might tell Raoul how nice it is to see him cuddling, feeding, and nurturing the baby, because some people in society do not believe that boys should be acting in such "feminine" ways.

In early childhood we have taken the ideas and concepts of gender equality and gender equity seriously and have used a variety of these strategies in our classrooms with the intent of confronting gender inequities. One of the most popular—and, at the time of its original publication, controversial—resources is Derman-Sparks' (1991) *Anti-Bias Curriculum: Tools for Empowering Children.* The teaching strategies found in this resource include expanding children's play options, expanding children's understanding of gender anatomy and gender identity, and expanding children's awareness of gender roles. These recommendations are based on socialization theories of learning, believing in the power of teachers to change children's understandings of gender bias.

Weaknesses of These Theories

Although it might be difficult to deny that biology has some impact on gender, and there is much evidence that people can shape their behavior through reinforcement and modeling, there are several weaknesses and limitations to explaining the construction of gender within these theories. These have been thoroughly analyzed by Bohan (1997); Browne (2004); Davies (2003); Fausto-Sterling (1992); Henriques, Hollway, Urwin, Venn, and Walkerdine (1984); Walkerdine (1990); and others. It is argued that we should move away from these essentializing theories of gender construction because they reduce all femininities and masculinities to a simple and particular way of being *either* a girl *or* a boy, and because they are unable to theorize power (Connell, 1987).

For some, socialization theories of gender imply that what men and women are *socially* is derived from what they are *biologically* (Davies, 2003; Lorber, 1994). This assumes that sexual differences are really biologically based and that the gender roles a child is taught are socially and superficially "placed over" the "real" biological differences. This view requires teachers to believe that children passively learn gender. That is, children learn gender-appropriate behaviors simply by watching and listening to others. In doing so, children are soaking up and accepting the gender messages they see and hear. The people doing the socializing are understood to be active, while the children obediently agree to all that is said and done. An example of this in practice would be if Raoul simply accepted all of his teacher's efforts at wanting him to be a more caring and nurturing sort of player. This is highly problematic, as it relies on popular notions of adult-child relations. Socialization theories assume that the older, bigger, and wiser adult has the power to control and mold the younger, smaller, and more naive child. This view fails to recognize that children are active, that they can make decisions and choices, and that they have the ability to resist and challenge adults (Davies, 2003). Anyone who has worked with children knows that it is highly unlikely that Raoul will simply comply with his teacher's wishes. Instead, he might snicker or laugh at her suggestions or strongly reply, "No, I don't want to do that. I want to be the bad guy!" Or his teacher might find that he simply stops going to the dramatic play area and instead plays aggressively and violently at times, when she is not looking. Finally, these theories of gender construction do not consider the possible effects that gender norms, or particular ways that society values being *either* a boy *or* a girl, might have on how we become gendered beings (Butler, 1990).

When thinking critically about biological and socialization theories of gender formation, we can begin questioning if these theories adequately explain why gender has developed in the way it has, why gender norms change over time, or why the meanings and practices of gender vary according to culture and race. For some of us, common views of gender are incomplete and unable to tell the whole gender story. These perspectives fail to acknowledge the complexities of relationships between individuals and the social worlds they live in, particularly children's abilities to distinguish for *themselves* ways in which the social world is organized and how they take an active part in the construction of gender by making choices about dominant and contradictory understandings of what it means to be female or male (Alloway, 1995; Davies, 2003; MacNaughton, 2000; Paechter, 1998).

New Ways for Seeing Gender

Several early childhood teachers and researchers do not accept these current arguments about gender, as they obscure a critical examination of gender differences in society (e.g., Davies, 2003; MacNaughton, 2000). This section will explore how postdevelopmental perspectives, such as feminist poststructuralism and queer theory, are used to challenge the Western cultural assumption that there is a direct, causal, and necessary connection between biological sex and the gender role one takes up (Connell, 1995; Nicholson, 1994; Paechter, 1998). Major concepts of poststructuralism, such as language, discourse, subjectivity, agency, and power will be discussed in order to show how feminist poststructuralism utilizes them to make sense of gender and why gender inequity exists. Adding to these complexities, this section will then introduce queer theory and show how it also challenges the field of early childhood to resist, rather than run away from, simplistic notions of gender.

Feminist Poststructuralism

Feminist poststructuralism developed from theories of poststructuralism and postmodernism (Weiner, 1994). Most scholars agree that the term *poststructuralism* does not refer to one general theory or have one fixed meaning. Instead, it is used to describe the mechanisms of power and how meaning and power are organized, enacted, and opposed in our society. Poststructuralism becomes feminist when matters of gender and a commitment to change are of central concern. Therefore, feminist poststructuralism is used throughout this book to understand the complexities of gender discourses in order to create opportunities for equity and justice in all children's lives (Weedon, 1997).

Feminist poststructuralism offers the field of early childhood education a way of producing new knowledge by using poststructural theories of language, discourse, subjectivity, and agency to understand how power is exercised in the classroom. In doing so, the gender terrain is exposed, showing how oppression works and how resisting gender inequities might be possible in the classroom. The next sections define these important poststructuralist concepts and show the possible ways they can be used in the classroom to create new ways of seeing and knowing classroom life.

Language Poststructuralism asserts that all meaning and knowledge are constituted through language, and language is the key to how we create meaning as socially constructed individuals. If meaning is created through language, then it is neither fixed nor essential. By seeing language as a social and political site of struggle, it becomes possible to conceptualize that language is where social meaning, power, and subjectivity are formed and are always open to challenges, redefinitions, rereadings, and reinterpretations (Weedon, 1997).

In the classroom this means that children are creating and re-creating meanings about gender through their talk and actions. Children are not simply being girls and boys; rather, through their talk with each other, they are taking an active part in constructing what it means to be a girl and a boy at a particular time and place. Sometimes children's talk and actions are reinforcing gender norms, such as when Alan exclaims, "Boys only play football and girls only are cheerleaders!" However, it is also possible that children are challenging and reinterpreting gender norms and ideals through their relationships in the classroom. So if Anne chooses to gender-bend at the dramatic play area, pretending to be a boy, she is not just copying how her older brother plays but is reinterpreting, at that particular moment, what it means to be a girl.

Discourse Discourse is not simply the use of words; rather, it is a broad concept used throughout this book to refer to a theoretical grid of power and knowledge, in which knowledge and power are integrated with each other and impossible to separate (Foucault, 1980a). Discourse is a structuring principle in the classroom and society, and language is always located in discourse. When combined with social practices, discourses constitute knowledge, subjectivities, and power relations (Weedon, 1997).

Discourse is a way of speaking, writing, thinking, feeling, or acting that incorporates particular ideas as "truths." Discourses provide a framework for how we think. They also carry messages about power and seek to establish a set of hidden rules about who has power and who does not, or who is right/normal and who is wrong/abnormal. Power, status, and privilege are constructed through discourse. Since language is located in discourse, discourses will also be transparent and open to multiple and contradictory meanings (Foucault, 1980a). In other words, how a teacher conceptualizes Sophie's gendered ways may be quite different from how Raoul understands, values, and desires Sophie's femininity. While a teacher might find Sophie's compliant behaviors troubling, Raoul may find them desirable.

Dominant discourses appear "natural," supporting and perpetuating existing power relations, tending to constitute the subjectivity of most people (Foucault, 1980a; Gavey, 1997; Weedon, 1997). These discourses have become so taken for granted, common, and unthreatening that they often prevent other ways of looking at being gendered (Paechter, 1998). As a result, thinking about gender in alternative ways becomes difficult. Both biological and socialization theories of gender differences can be considered the dominant discourses for understanding how children become gendered. Since these ways of conceptualizing gender are based on common scientific "facts," it would not be considered ordinary practice for teachers to question children's gendered behaviors. If children are born this way or socialized by their families, why bother?

Feminist poststructuralism is interested in how particular discourses operate to normalize gender, and for feminist poststructuralists, this is considered a source of inequity. Feminist poststructuralism becomes a tool that allows teachers to recognize the multiple discourses circulating in the classroom and how children are constituted, positioned, and marginalized through them. These ways of understanding the social terrain of the classroom make it possible for teachers to see children differently and to understand why Raoul finds Sophie and her actions desirable, and why Sophie chooses to take up particular gender discourses. Understanding discourses and how they work in classroom settings is a vital and necessary step toward understanding how gender is socially constructed and contested. As a result of this new knowledge, teachers can begin the difficult task of imagining new discourses in which children can be situated as neither female nor male, but as human beings (Davies, 2003).

Subjectivity Subjectivity refers to an individual's conscious and unconscious thoughts, sense of self, and understanding of one's relation to the world. A person's subjectivity is a process that is socially and actively constructed through discourses and language. The concept of subjectivity is different from the concept of identity, as it shifts our attention away from thinking of individuals as rational, unified, and universal beings and toward focusing on how our everyday experiences are often shifting and sometimes fragmented (Davies, 2003; Gavey, 1997; Weedon, 1997).

The concept of subjectivity offers the possibility of understanding the contradictory nature of human beings. Different discourses, such as gender, provide for a range of subjectivities for us to take up, allowing individuals to be positioned or to position themselves in a variety of ways. For example, Sophie is not simply one kind of girl; rather, she experiences multiple subjectivities (or ways of being a girl) during the school day. While in music, sitting quietly in her new dress, raising her hand to ask questions, and delicately playing the triangle, she is referred to by the teacher as a "nice," "good," and "pretty" student. These comments help create the discourse of the classroom, positioning Sophie as a certain kind of female student in music class. At the same time Sophie is choosing to take up and perform this form of femininity. Thirty minutes later, during center time, Sophie is happily making Barbie cards at the paper work table with two other girls. At this moment in time, while situated within this social context, with this particular group of girls, her feminized play positions her as powerful. The girls ask Sophie about her Barbie dolls, how she dresses them, the accessories she has for them, and so on. Then during work share, a time in the day when children share the work that they did during center time, as she begins talking about the Barbie cards she made, a group of boys publicly laugh at her work and she is instantly devalued and positioned as powerless. When outside at recess, Sophie sits off to the side, neither playing chase nor swinging upside down on the bars. When asked why she is not playing, she explains, "I don't want to get my new outfit messy and the boys can see my panties if I hang upside down on the bars." Finally, while walking up the stairs with her line partner, Sophie suddenly stops, places her hands on her hips, and loudly states, "You are gross and ugly. I don't want to touch your hand!" These are just a few examples of how Sophie's subjectivity is shifting, changing, and at times contradictory. Sophie is not just a sweet, innocent, and cute girl; she can also be mean, compliant, rude, and marginalized.

Agency The concept of agency is concerned with an individual's ability to make choices, control events, and be powerful. According to Davies (2004), agency is also one's capacity to resist, subvert, and change discourses. And yet agency is not about an individual's autonomy, because one's subjectivity is always embedded within a social context. Following this line of argument includes the idea that agency is not something that individuals possess or a theoretical idea, but is always produced by the gaps opened up in regulatory norms or through power. Traditional early childhood discourses often position young children as naive, passive, and powerless, making children's agency difficult to recognize. This perspective opens up the possibility that children actively resist a teacher's good intentions toward equity.

Power This book draws upon the work of Foucault's (1980a, 1980b) theories of power. From this perspective, power is envisioned as a relation or process operating in our social world, rather than as something possessed by individuals. Power operates within all relationships and is expressed through discourse. Therefore, Foucault (1980b) argues for analyses that understand power as something that circulates and at the same time constructs individuals. For Foucault and feminist poststructuralists who use his work, "individuals are the vehicles of power, not its points of application" (p. 98). From this perspective, it becomes important to understand how power works, or the strategies, tactics, and techniques of power, not simply who has or does not have power. The previous example of how Sophie experiences multiple subjectivities also provides a glimpse of how power works. There are moments in which she experiences powerful gender relations (i.e., when she is creating the Barbie cards), and at other times she is positioned as powerless (i.e., when the boys publicly laugh at her feminine interests). Sophie does not own the power; rather, her knowledge of Barbie is one strategy that she uses to wield power with the girls. Additionally, since the boys know the dominant discourse about gender and where boys and girls stand, they are the only ones who can criticize Sophie's Barbie pictures, positioning her as powerless.

Foucault (1980b) argues that power and knowledge are interrelated and strongly influence each other. Power relations exist within fields of knowledge, or "regimes of truth," which produce and exercise particular forms of power relations. By examining power as a relation and in its local forms, such as the kindergarten classroom, it is possible to understand the ways in which the gendered social order is structured and regulated.

Gender A feminist poststructuralist perspective on gender is based on poststructuralist concepts of language, discourse, subjectivity, agency, and power. This point of view sees gender as a political, dynamic, and social construction. Feminist poststructuralism does not believe that gender is simply a trait of individuals that they are either born with or socialized into, but rather that gender is a social construct that identifies particular transactions that are understood to be appropriate to one sex (Bohan, 1997). This perspective focuses on the social and relational aspects of gender, recognizing how gender resides in context and how it is constructed through children's talk, actions, and interactions with each other and the social world (Thorne, 1995; Bohan, 1997). Social relationships become more important in the construction of gender and are seen as interactive and inseparable. Subsequently, teachers working from this perspective notice and begin questioning the interactions, acts, and relations among children

(Thorne, 1995; Bohan, 1997). In doing so, issues of power are revealed, and it becomes possible to see how gender is constructed through power relations and then, presumably, attempt to intervene. A feminist poststructuralist analysis of gender illuminates the role of power in the construction of subjectivities and how it subordinates and marginalizes both girls and boys (Flax, 1990).

Feminist poststructuralism also sees girls as being multiply located and variously positioned in the classroom. Instead of being rational, unified subjects, human beings have multiple identities. There is no single way to be; rather, there are multiple gender identities that we choose to take up. This also implies that instead of seeing girls as powerless and disadvantaged in school, attention should turn toward analyzing how girls experience gender relations in the classroom. Striving to understand girls' situations and positions, in connection to the patriarchal power relations they are experiencing, becomes the teacher's responsibility (Flax, 1990; MacNaughton, 1997).

In summary, feminist poststructuralism is an alternative theoretical perspective that opens up new ways for understanding teaching, learning, and children. Language, discourse, subjectivity, agency, and power can be used to uncover the complexities of gender and how children take an active part in understanding gender and constructing it for themselves and others.

Queer Theory

Emerging from gay, lesbian, and bisexual studies, queer theorists contend that gender equity can come about only through a radical change in our conventional notions of understanding gender (Warner, 1993; Phelan, 1997). By using feminist poststructuralist theories of language, discourse, subjectivity, agency, and power to formulate new understandings of gender, queer theorists have been critically analyzing heterosexuality and its position in the social construction of gender (Butler, 1990; Connell, 1987, 1996; Rich, 1980; Sedgwick, 1990). By recognizing and questioning concepts of normalization and privileges found within heterosexual culture, queer theory helps deepen understandings of the social construction of gender (Britzman, 1995; Warner, 1993).

Hegemonic Masculinity and Emphasized Femininity In their efforts to understand and challenge existing power relations between males and females, queer theorists are exploring heterosexuality as a form of sexism and social regulation (Connell, 1987; Warner, 1993). This perspective believes that every culture has hegemonic or morally dominant forms of genders and sexualities that are considered right or proper for women and men (Lorber, 1994). The word *hegemony* is often defined as the domination of one group over another (Gramsci, 1971). Hegemonic masculinity, as defined by Connell (1987, 1996), is the cultural expression of the dominant form of masculinity that regulates and subordinates other patterns of masculinity and femininity. In the kindergarten classroom, hegemonic masculinity can be thought of as the most desirable and powerful way to be a boy. The most important feature of hegemonic masculinity is heterosexuality, which shapes the structural order of all gender relations (Connell, 1987).

According to Connell's (1987) understandings of femininity and masculinity, there is no femininity in our present society that is hegemonic. Instead, there is a type of femininity called emphasized femininity, which is defined around the compliance with subordination and is oriented around accommodating the interests and desires of men. In other words, emphasized femininity does not regulate other forms of femininities, but is always constructed in relation to hegemonic masculinity. "Hegemonic" and "emphasized" signify positions of cultural authority, not total dominance, therefore allowing other forms of femininities and masculinities to persist (Connell, 1996). Both hegemonic masculinity and emphasized femininity maintain practices that institutionalize men's dominance over women, or in this case boys' dominance over girls. As a result, the gendered social order is regulated by the children *themselves* as they take an active part in the gendering process.

These dominant forms of hegemonic masculinity and emphasized femininity are influenced by heterosexual discourses, which are defined as stereotypical gendered norms and expectations considered appropriately female and male, including society's expectations of males and females to fall in love and sexually desire a member of the opposite sex. Additionally, not only are males and females expected to desire the opposite sex, but also it is assumed that a certain kind of femininity "belongs" or "goes" with a particular kind of masculinity. This idea reinforces the relational aspects of how gender is socially constructed. For example, the stereotypical ways that Raoul and Alan violently and aggressively played might be considered by Sophie and Anne as desirable gender performances.

The Heterosexual Matrix A queer perspective sees gender as a kind of becoming or activity performed normatively, making it impossible to understand gender except through what Butler (1990) calls the "heterosexual matrix," a term used to "designate that grid of cultural intelligibility through which bodies, genders, and desires are naturalized" (p. 151). In other words, the heterosexual matrix regulates gender and gender relations so that heterosexuality becomes the "normal," right, and only way to be.

Like feminist poststructuralism, a queer understanding of gender moves away from theories of gender construction that assume sex determines gender. Instead, gender is seen as a performance. Gender performativity is not about choosing which gender one will be on a particular day; rather, it is about the effects of repeating, performing, and embodying gender norms through language and actions. As a social construction, gender is based on "compulsory heterosexuality" (Butler, 1990). The concept of genderedness becomes meaningless in the absence of heterosexuality as an institution. To understand gender it is necessary to realize the power and pervasiveness of heterosexuality. Queer theorists believe that heterosexuality is compulsory and enforced both through rewards for appropriate gendered and heterosexual behaviors and through punishments for deviations from the conventional or "normal" ways of being a girl or a boy. Heterosexual behaviors are treated as normal throughout the school day. For instance, when teachers read stories during group time, they rarely question whether the adult female and male characters in the stories are married. Rather, it is simply assumed that they are. Heterosexual behaviors are reinforced as teachers observe from the sidelines when children are playing "princess" at the dramatic play area and simply smile or laugh when commenting how cute the girls are as they get ready to go out dancing with the prince. A queer understanding of gender assumes that heterosexuality functions to produce "normal" understandings of masculinity and femininity, implying that heterosexism, prejudice by heterosexuals against homosexuals, is another form of sexism that is often overlooked in the classroom.

Heterosexual Discourses As a form of sexism, heterosexuality is neither natural nor freely chosen, but rather a political institution that disempowers women and other marginalized populations (Rich, 1980). It is important to remember that these critiques of heterosexism are not attacks on heterosexual practices per se, but rather the discourses of heterosexuality and how they have become embedded into the foundations of our thoughts; subsequently manifesting and maintaining power over females and others (Butler, 1990; Rich, 1980; Sedgwick, 1990).

In the early childhood classroom, heterosexual norms are viewed as regulatory when they encourage children to maintain their gendered roles. Often teachers and children idealize heterosexual norms without noticing how these actions maintain gender inequity. For example, girls might be expected, by both genders, to enact passivity and compliance in order to be desirable to boys. Or boys might be presumed to exhibit dominant and aggressive roles in order to be liked by their peers. Understanding gender through the heterosexual matrix opens up new ways for seeing gender and children's attachment to stereotypical gendered differences. This point of view encourages teachers to discover why children desire to take up oppressive gender roles in their play. It also becomes possible for teachers to uncover how discourses of heterosexuality regulate the gendered social order of the classroom. As a result of these new understandings of gender, how children are doing gender in the classroom takes on a different set of meanings, as does the role of the early childhood teacher. These perspectives encourage teachers to question the ways young children are playing it straight in the classroom and how this may impact gender equity for girls and boys.

Rereading the Play Scenario in New Ways

Taking into consideration both feminist poststructuralist understandings of gender and queer theory's questions about compulsory heterosexuality, how might a teacher see children's play now?

Raoul: Where are you going today?

Alan: I'm going to kill some people. I'm a villain.

Raoul: (Uses a plastic banana as a gun and starts shooting at Alan) Bang, pow, pow, pow! I got you!

Alan: Hey, Raoul . . . my name is Bond . . . James Bond (lowering his head toward the floor while looking up with his eyes).

Sophie: *Guys, g:u:y:s* . . . We need a table. (Using a high-pitched and singsong voice. She is standing with her feet apart and with both hands on her hips.)

Alan: We can make it later.

Sophie: (Talking into the phone) No, we are eating right now. (Turns to Anne) He's asleep. Someone shot him.

Anne: He said, "I'm afraid." He has pain. We need to check if the bullet is in his heart.

Referring again to our play scenario, a teacher working from a feminist poststructuralist and queer perspective would immediately notice the social aspect of the play and how children's gender resides within a political and social context. Anne, Sophie, Raoul, and Alan's talk and actions no longer are viewed as innocent, but rather are seen to play a major part in the gendering process. Instead of viewing this play as cute or innocent, the teacher focuses her inquiries on the hard work that these children are doing at creating and re-creating gender. By moving away from the idea that children are born with certain distinct gendered behaviors, teachers are able to see how children are active and powerful players in the classroom as they talk and interact with gender discourses and each other. For instance, when Raoul and Alan play James Bond, they are embodying and re-creating one form of masculinity for themselves, and as Sophie and Anne watch and listen, this way of being a boy is performed for them. All of these players are taking an active part in constructing what it means to be a girl and what it means to be a boy. Alan did not simply incorporate James Bond into his play, but rather deliberately chose to be James Bond because of the power and prestige the character represents. A teacher might consider how Raoul and Alan's play is constructing both femininities and masculinities in the classroom.

Feminist poststructuralist and queer perspectives uncover how these four children use their understandings of what it means to be a girl or boy to actively reinforce gender norms. For example, from the beginning of their play, it is assumed that the boys will be leaving the house to take part in action-packed and aggressive events, such as capturing and killing the bad guys, while the girls will be staying home to cook. Within seconds, the girls take on the responsibility of tending to a gunshot victim apparently caught in the boys' crossfire. Referring to himself as James Bond, wanting to kill and to be a villain, Alan is choosing to position himself within a particular masculine discourse. As a result of the boys' play, Sophie and Anne are positioned as submissive and nurturing females as both take care of the wounded gunshot victim. Even the way that Sophie physically positions her body and uses her voice can be read as a gender performance. By using a high-pitched and singsong voice, and accentuating her hips as she places both hands on them, she embodies and enacts a certain form of femininity that gets the attention of the boys. Not only is Sophie playing it straight, but as she chooses to do a particular gender performance, she is constructing her gender in relation to hegemonic masculinity.

Teachers using alternative perspectives to make sense of children's talk and actions might consider the gender discourses that are circulating in the classroom and how they are working to position boys and girls in relationship to each other. A teacher might discover that these discourses support more play options for the boys, while the girls are limited in what they can do. An awareness of the dominant gender discourses and how they work in the classroom could be a catalyst for rethinking the early childhood curriculum. As the children continue playing it straight in the dramatic play center, the following transpires:

Alan: Okay, let's make the table.

Sophie: Okay.

Alan: We are going to make the table now.

Sophie: We . . . are going to have dinner.

Alan: Let's go out to dinner.

Sophie: I'm not going to drive.

Alan: (To Raoul) Get in the car. Now! (A plastic banana is stuffed in his pants. He takes a set of keys out of his pocket. Then he reaches into his pants for the banana, pulls it out, and uses it as a gun, making shooting sounds.)

Raoul: (Opening up a makeup box and looking into it) I need a gun.

Sophie: *Wow, guys,* we are going out to dinner (smiling). We don't have to cook (placing both hands on her cheeks). But I'm not going to have to cook.

Raoul: (Waiting in the car) Alan, we have to go to dinner.

Alan: I'm not going.

Raoul: (To Sophie) Are you ready?

Sophie: I have to get ready. It will take me a few minutes.

As the macho and hegemonic male, Alan makes all of the decisions and controls the play. For example, Alan tells Sophie that he will make the table, decides that they will go out to dinner, orders Raoul to get into the car, and changes his mind about going out to dinner. Furthermore, Alan's action of reaching into his pants to pull out a weapon might be interpreted as a symbol of sexual power and shows how hegemonic masculinity marginalizes other ways of being a boy. Sophie's suggestion of having dinner can be seen as a form of resistance, as she momentarily has the slim chance of controlling the play. That is, if they were going to have dinner, she would get to decide what and when they eat. However, the power relationship quickly shifts as Alan regains control by restating his wish to go out to dinner. Instead of resisting Alan's suggestion, Sophie's tone of voice, expressions, and gestures indicate that she is quite excited about getting out of the house and going out to dinner. Unfortunately, Sophie can't just go. Instead, she finds it necessary to "get ready," implying that girls have to worry about how they look before leaving the house and entering the public realm of restaurants. This exchange between Sophie and

Alan shows how gendered power relationships quickly shift and change, and how they rely on discourses.

Since feminist poststructuralism and queer theory see gender differently than biological and socialization perspectives do, new and complex understandings about the gendering process are beginning to reveal themselves. For instance, Anne, Sophie, Raoul, and Alan did not merely soak up gender-appropriate ways to play, but instead took an active part in teaching each other and learning for themselves how to be girls and boys as they play it "straight," negotiating their way through gender power relationships and discourses. Although Sophie learned another lesson in being powerless, she is also learning the need to contest this power differently next time. By shifting away from the idea that Sophie and Anne are disadvantaged in their play, teachers will need to analyze how these girls experience gender relations and power in the classroom before taking action.

Uncovering the Heterosexual Matrix

Continuing to use feminist poststructuralism and queer theory as tools for seeing gender in the classroom makes the heterosexual matrix apparent.

> As their play continues, Alan and Raoul persist in shooting each other with a set of plastic keys and the banana. Raoul begins jumping out of and back into the car. Sophie pulls a blue dress out of the dress-up box and asks an adult in the classroom to help zip it up.

Alan: (To Raoul) We are taking the two ladies to dinner.

Sophie: Sister is getting ready for dinner. It will take a bit of time. You will have to wait. (Finds some costume jewelry and puts on a pair of earrings. She then grabs a silver purse, slings it over her shoulder, walks over to the full-length mirror, and looks at herself. She begins "posing" for the mirror.)

Anne: (Trying on a pair of earrings while looking at herself in the mirror of the small plastic makeup box)

Sophie: (Puts on a necklace, bracelet, and scarf) I'm just going to be ready in two minutes, guys!

Raoul: (Wrestling with Alan. They begin doing karate moves and shooting each other with the plastic banana and car keys.)

Sophie: Guys (loudly and with hands on both hips) . . . I thought we were going to dinner?

Alan: We are, I'm just fixing the car. We need to go.

Sophie: I'm all ready now. (She is smiling while extending both arms out. She swings her hips back and forth and then twirls around.)

Sheila: (An adult classroom volunteer. She notices Sophie from across the room and purposefully comes over.) Sophie, I love your dress! You look so pretty!

Sophie: (Sits in the backseat of the car, and Alan is driving. Alan and Raoul start wrestling and shooting each other, and a few blocks that are a part of the car get knocked down. Their voices are getting louder. The banana gun appears, and shooting starts.) Eeeeeeeeeeeeek! (High-pitched shriek. She also places her hands over her eyes while smiling.)

Anne: Boys!

Alan: Officer, you need to get out of here. This BMW is a mess.

Holly: (Has noticed the play from the paper work center and comes over to watch) You look so:o:o:o beautiful Sophie.

Raoul: (Starts jumping into and out of the car)

Sophie: Eeeeeeeeeeeeek! (High-pitched scream, with a smile)

Anne: (To Sophie) Don't scare me like that. (Sits on the floor) Mom, I got hurt and I can't get up. Can you help me? (She is on the floor)

Alan works hard to shift the play toward the exciting and action-filled world outside of the home. In doing so, all four players are situated within the heterosexual matrix, requiring Sophie and Anne to exhibit emphasized femininity and Raoul and Alan to display forms of hegemonic masculinity. Immediately, the girls talk about getting ready and begin transforming themselves for their big night out. Sophie puts on a special outfit, complete with a range of accessories. She presents herself as an object as she proudly poses for the mirror and extends both of her hands out wide, as if to say, "Here I am!" Anne excitedly tries on a sparkly pair of earrings and admires them in the mirror. Sophie's appearance is noticed first by an adult volunteer in the class and then by Holly, a classmate. Both are reinforcing the importance of looking beautiful for boys.

While observing this play, a teacher working from a feminist poststructuralist and queer perspective might notice that all four children seem to take on appropriate gender roles with delight. That is, the boys are enjoying wrestling, doing karate moves, and shooting each other. Although the girls are shrieking, their smiles and actions are full of energy and excitement. All of the children are enjoying a chance to demonstrate their gender competence. They feel good while playing the heterosexual game. At one point during the play, Sophie abruptly stops and reprimands the boys' violent actions by using a loud (some might say unladylike) voice, placing her hands on her hips to show the boys that she is serious and means business. Sophie is trying to gain more power by accessing female adult discourses. In response, Alan reassures her that he is fixing the car and tells her that they need to go. Alan is showing Sophie that he is a serious male, not just a violent one. By leaving the house, Alan will have more of a chance to gain his power back, as he takes part in the world of action and fast cars.

Raising New Questions About Gender and Power

These alternative frameworks encourage teachers to question how children are experiencing gender and power. Subsequently, a teacher may wonder about the following:

- Was Sophie experiencing a moment of power when she reprimanded the boys?
- Is she beginning to think about resisting the expectation that girls are scared and helpless when playing these action-filled games with the boys?

- Does she find this kind of play exciting? Why or why not?
- How do these particular forms of femininity make Sophie feel?
- Are some forms of femininity more exciting than others?
- How are gender discourses defining what it means to be a girl or a boy in this classroom?
- How are these gender discourses constructing, positioning, and marginalizing Sophie, Anne, Alan, and Raoul?
- How do Sophie and Anne work together to create forms of femininity?
- How do Alan and Raoul work together to create forms of masculinity?
- If all of these discourses are circulating in the classroom and children are actively taking them up, then what should the teacher do?
- How can the teacher provide opportunities for the children to experience power and powerful relationships?

Recommendations for Practice

Both feminist poststructualism and queer theory open up alternative pathways for thinking about how children become gendered, making it possible to rethink, create, and invent gender equity strategies that are able to confront and change the current gendered social order of the classroom. If, as these play scenarios suggest, children not only are socialized into dominant gendered ways of behaving, but are active in and through their own culture of creating particular gendered social orders, then teachers have to rethink their actions in the classroom. It is probably not enough simply to understand children through developmental domains. Instead, teachers must draw from a range of theoretical perspectives to understand the complexities of classroom life and what children are learning about gender. Instead of blaming inequity and bias on children, parents, teachers, television, popular culture, or the early childhood curriculum, we must look deeply at the gender discourses available to children and how they are being used. As a result, it becomes possible to look differently at the ways children are doing gender in the classroom, including how some children resist a teacher's attempts to change their gendered behaviors.

Teacher Interventions New understandings of gender make it imperative for teachers to intervene more overtly in children's play by questioning and challenging their gendered assumptions. Such interactions might include stepping into children's play to question their gendered practices. For example, a classroom teacher working from a feminist poststructuralist and queer perspective would not let Sophie, Anne, Alan, and Raoul's play just happen. Instead, she would engage the children in critical dialogue about their play. She might step in and ask Raoul why he likes to be James Bond and how it makes him feel to be this character. She would also consider asking Sophie if she likes James Bond and why. This intervention may then lead to a discussion with Sophie, Anne, Alan, and Raoul about the different ways that they can be girls and boys in their play, with the teacher asking them which ways they like best to play and why.

Another possible intervention includes developing spaces in the classroom and curriculum for children to practice resisting dominant gender norms. After holding large and small group discussions around gender bending, the class might decide on particular times when anyone can gender-bend safely in the classroom. Follow-up discussions might uncover what it felt like to pretend to be the opposite gender, and what was easy or hard about this kind of play. Or, in the case of the play scenario, the teacher might ask Sophie about her desire to go out to dinner and why she wanted to do this. Or the teacher might inquire when Sophie attempted to stop the aggressive play that she found herself a part of. These play scenarios could then be replayed, and Sophie could be given the opportunity to safely resist the gender norms—an effort that might have been too difficult to carry out on her own.

Accepting the Challenge

This chapter began by questioning the relevance of relying exclusively on child development to inform practice in early childhood education, showing how postdevelopmental perspectives are used to understand teaching, learning, and children. Feminist poststructuralism and queer theory were explored, highlighting how they can bring about new ways of understanding children's gendered identities and early childhood teaching.

Chapter 2 explains how I researched *with* children in the kindergarten classroom in order to create new understandings about the ways in which they were taking an active part in the social construction of gender. I describe the learning community, present the multiple qualitative methods used for collecting data, and discuss the role I played as a participant observer. I also address how feminist poststructuralism supports a self-reflective research design, including how data analysis was used to locate the heterosexual matrix in the classroom. This chapter is important since the actions and outcomes of children do not occur in a vacuum. The context of the classroom is critical because it impacts not only on what data is collected but also on the nature of analysis.

Since the heterosexual matrix is fundamental to the social construction of gender, Chapter 3 provides an in-depth look at how gender discourses operate throughout the early childhood classroom, and how children used their understandings of these discourses to influence gender. This chapter provides more detail of how feminist poststructuralism and queer theory are used to make sense of the complexities of classroom life, highlighting the social context of the classroom and what children are learning about gender. Not only do young children know that there are certain, desirable, and "normal" ways to be either a girl or a boy, but they also realize that sometimes gender is not so black and white but is full of contradictions and ambiguities.

Building on the theoretical concepts put forth in Chapter 3, Chapters 4, 5, and 6 are three case studies showing how an Anglo-American middle-class boy, an Anglo-American working-class girl, and an Asian American middle-class girl actively do gender in their kindergarten classroom. These case studies show not only how young children maintain gender norms, but also how they resist and subvert them as well. Queer theory and feminist poststructuralist concepts of language, discourse, subjectivity, agency, and power are used to explore some of the assumptions we hold about children's identities (Sears, 1999). These case studies will help teachers to see how alternative perspectives can be used to understand the complexities of gender and classroom life in new ways.

The final chapter begins the process of reconceptualizing early childhood teaching. If feminist poststructuralism and queer theory are used to rethink gender, then we need to consider what kinds of new pedagogies are needed to address and challenge gender norms in practice. This chapter takes up Tobin's (1997) call for "queering appropriate practice" (p. 33) in early childhood as it puts forth queer possibilities that move toward challenging categorical thinking, promoting interpersonal intelligence, and fostering a critical consciousness in the early childhood classroom.

For some teachers, these ways of thinking about young children and teaching will be new and exciting. For others, it will seem strange, unfamiliar, and probably daunting. It is important to realize that moving away from a foundation based on child development toward the unfamiliar terrain of postdevelopmentalism is neither easy nor comfortable. It is always difficult to teach against the dominant discourses of early childhood education. Like some of the children in this book, who take risks in their gender work, there are teachers who take risks when they engage in questioning, rethinking, and challenging dominant discourses, such as the knowledge base of early childhood education and common understandings of gender. But for those teachers and children committed to equity and social justice, this kind of work is not just risky, but also necessary. We need to consider the ramifications if teachers and children don't question and challenge the status quo. How can the field of early childhood education afford not to contemplate alternative ways of knowing, understanding, and learning? Life in the twenty-first century is complex, and questioning our practices is essential. DAP is a product of a different era and social conditions. It is now necessary to consider new ways for understanding gender, children, learning, and teaching. Difficult questions will be posed in the process of challenging oneself to see what feminist poststructuralism and queer theory offer and how this impacts practice and ways of thinking about teaching. These questions may not always have clear-cut answers but they are a necessary part of creating a new knowledge base in early childhood education.

2

RESEARCHING WITH CHILDREN
IN THE EARLY CHILDHOOD
CLASSROOM

This chapter describes the learning community, including the curriculum, the teacher, and the children, involved in this investigation of gender in an early childhood classroom. It considers the multiple qualitative methods used for collecting information about the everyday practices of the classroom and the role of a participant observer in the process. The ways in which feminist poststructuralism supports self-reflective research are addressed, including how critical discourse analysis can be used as a tool for seeing how broader forms of discourse and power are manifested in everyday texts (Gavey, 1997; Hicks, 1995–96; Luke, 1995; MacNaughton, 1998). Ways of interpreting classroom observations are explained, particularly how the heterosexual matrix was systematically located in this classroom.

The Learning Community

The kindergarten studied was part of a small, progressive, alternative public elementary school located in a northeastern urban city in the

United States and will be referred to as Public School (PS) 99. A group of teachers started this school in 1991 as an "option school" (a school founded upon a specific idea or philosophy). PS 99 is considered child-centered, and its educational philosophy is based on a learner-centered and inquiry-based process approach to teaching and learning. The curriculum emphasizes real-world problem solving, building lifelong literacies, and fostering a love of language and the arts. The school is also an established national demonstration site for the whole-language and process approach to teaching and learning.

Within the educational community, PS 99 is highly regarded, and several partnerships with schools of education have been established. Preservice teachers from several universities are placed in these classrooms for their field experiences. It is common for classrooms to have three and four preservice teachers at a time.

The staff is composed of expert and experienced teachers who serve as mentors in citywide educational programs, staff developers, cooperating teachers, and national consultants. Several of these teachers are published authors, writing and researching on topics such as integrative curriculum, literacy in the classroom, and the reading and writing process. These teachers see themselves as both teacher researchers and teacher educators. The school's philosophy, teaching techniques, and teachers are well documented in videos, textbooks, and professional and academic journals. Although children come from all over the city to attend PS 99, most of the student body lives in the surrounding neighborhood. At the time of the investigation, the school had 527 students and 29 teachers. Serving a diverse student population, PS 99 educated children from 32 countries, with 41 different languages being spoken at home.

The Classroom

There were 26 children in the kindergarten classroom, 18 girls and 8 boys. The children were ethnically and socioeconomically diverse, with 14 students categorized as middle-class and the remainder viewed as being working-class. In addition, there were one female teacher, one part-time female teaching assistant, and two female preservice teachers. I thought that this would be a useful classroom for investigating gender in alternative ways for two main reasons. First, emphasis and value were placed on play and language within the curriculum. Second and most important, this teacher was comfortable with having a researcher in her classroom for an entire school year to conduct an inquiry on gender.

My observations led me to view this classroom as child-centered and developmentally appropriate. The teacher's practices and the curriculum were influenced by the principles of child development. Following developmentally appropriate guidelines, this teacher believes that children learn best through play and by interacting with materials, other children, and adults (Bredekamp & Copple, 1997). Play was a regular part of this kindergarten classroom, and children had an opportunity to play during center time, which made up 60 minutes of their daily classroom routine. During center time, children are provided opportunities to work and play in the learning centers of their choice. The learning centers in this classroom include the easel, blocks, art table, paper-work table, wet-sand table, dry-sand table, table toys, dollhouse, dramatic play, discovery table, and reading on the rug.

Classroom routines include several literacy activities such as reading with older story partners three times a week, storytelling, singing, reading on the rug, writing workshop, and show-and-tell. The teacher uses a morning meeting to formally begin the school day. She also uses this time to introduce new concepts or month-long investigative projects. After center time there is usually a work share period, which includes the teacher selecting individual or small groups of children to share the work they did during center time. Sometimes work share consists of an individual child sharing her or his Lego construction or easel painting, while other times a group of children are asked to report about the story lines they created and enacted at dramatic play. Once a week, the class leaves the school building with the two other kindergarten classes to visit a nearby park. The class also leaves the classroom to participate in science, physical education, Spanish, art, music, and a performing arts program called Ta-Da.

An important aspect of this research is the belief that play constitutes real, here-and-now social worlds for children. Play is viewed as children's serious real-life work of constructing, organizing, and shaping social orders, and gender is recognized as one type of social order (Danby, 1998; Davies, 2003). By theorizing children as competent players in their social worlds, this inquiry believes that children have the ability to establish gendered practices and identities in their play (Davies, 2003). This classroom was eminently suitable for my research since it has an emphasis on play and provides children with a wide range of opportunities to read, write, and talk about their interests and desires. These qualities made it possible to locate, observe, and record gender discourses operating within a variety of activities occurring in a kindergarten classroom.

The Teacher

The kindergarten teacher, Isabel, has been teaching in the field of early childhood education for over twenty years and views herself not just as a teacher of children but also as a researcher and a teacher educator. As a researcher, Isabel continuously collects information about her practice through observations; talking with children, their families, and her colleagues; and collecting children's work samples. Isabel analyzes the data and discusses emerging themes with colleagues and preservice teachers. She strives to continuously improve her practice through critical reflection. For example, at the beginning of the school year, she was working on the idea of negotiation and the ways in which children resolve their transitions into the kindergarten classroom and the larger school community at PS 99. By closely observing children and families as they enter the classroom and prepare for the morning meeting, Isabel began seeing mornings as "thresholds" through which children negotiate their entrances into the classroom. Isabel deepens her inquiries by collecting children's writings, drawings, and narratives in order to illustrate and talk about negotiations and transitions with parents.

Isabel is also an early childhood teacher educator. As a mentor teacher, she makes a large contribution to the field of early childhood education by sharing her practices, insights, and understandings about research, theory, and teaching with the preservice teachers who work in her classroom. Since the school is nationally recognized, teachers from other elementary schools, school districts, states, and countries often visit, and therefore I was able to observe Isabel interacting with other educators from a range of settings. Additionally, Isabel occasionally taught early childhood courses at a local college.

Isabel values and cherishes teaching, researching, and collaborating with others. From the instant we met, Isabel welcomed me into her classroom and seemed excited about being a part of my research project. When asked what her thoughts were about research and having a researcher in her classroom, she replied:

> It's just part of all the other research. They [the children] know that you are a researcher because they see you taking notes and documenting and they understand that they are researchers and they take notes and document and observe. So you are one more in the community that is doing an inquiry.

Isabel intentionally creates an environment that supports a community of inquiry. She often uses research language in her practice, referring to the children as "researchers" and their everyday classroom work as "research," and encourages the children to do likewise. For example, an assortment of Beanie Babies, small collectible stuffed animals, was placed at the discovery table for approximately three weeks. During center time, children who chose to go to this center were asked to observe the stuffed animals and document their observations on a piece of paper. Isabel would then choose four or five children's documentations to be discussed during work share. She would ask each child to discuss her or his individual observations of the stuffed animals as well as to compare her or his observations with those of the other children.

From the beginning of this project, I shared my research agenda with Isabel. I advised her that I would be taking on the role of a participant observer while conducting a qualitative, flexible, and emergent research study of gender. I asked Isabel why she had so readily agreed to have me, a stranger, come and do research in her classroom. Her response indicates that she was interested in gender issues and viewed research as a collaborative endeavor.

> Because it interests me that someone is doing research on gender, but I think another reason is the way you presented yourself and your ideas and the way you made your request was very personal. I wouldn't have anyone in our classroom that makes us objects. I can see the dynamics of you working in a scientific way

for the purposes of your study and the balancing of the personal within that. It's interesting for me to watch that. It's interesting for me to be a part of your thoughts. But it wouldn't have happened if you're not who you are.

Isabel talked about Paolo Freire (1994), Lev Vygotsky (1986), and Garth Boomer (1992) influencing her beliefs about teaching and learning. The ideas put forth by these scholars have been incorporated into Isabel's practice—her interactions with children, the curriculum, and the way she creates the classroom environment. Isabel regards learning as being socially constructed and therefore invents classroom structures, rituals, and routines that enable and support social interactions between children. As a result, it is evident that the children themselves co-construct knowledge as they talk and interact with one another. Isabel believes that children come into the classroom with a range of experiences, and as they interact with each other or the classroom materials they learn. While talking with Isabel about the social construction of gender, I discovered how her views about gender coincide with her beliefs about learning.

> I think my students are learning who they are through their social interactions with each other, they are constructing their social being and they're constructing their literacies and their understandings in every cognitive sense. And I want that to happen between the learners and myself as one of the people in the learning community, and my student [preservice] teachers, so that it's not delivered.

At first, Isabel appears to be a progressive, developmentally appropriate early childhood teacher. A quick glance around the classroom indicates that she has created a learning environment that looks and sounds like a typical developmentally appropriate early childhood classroom. That is, children have opportunities to interact with materials and others, a large part of the school day is devoted to play, and the curriculum supports children's individual needs. However, a closer analysis into Isabel's theories about learning, teaching, and young children reveals a more radical approach to early childhood education. Overhearing Isabel explaining to Hazel, one of the preservice teachers in her class, how she purposely creates classroom structures and routines to promote interdependence between children rather than independence helped me recognize Isabel as a postdevelopmental teacher. Her aim, unlike that of many early childhood teachers, is not to have a classroom full of "26 little autonomous, independent workers, but rather 26 students who work together, supporting each other's learning." Although Isabel uses her knowledge of child development to plan for children, as a postdevelopmental teacher, she does not rely exclusively on this framework to inform her practice. The physical environment is a manifestation of this. For instance, none of the learning centers is designed for children to visit alone. Instead, all the centers have room for at least two children so that they are able to talk, negotiate, and learn from each other.

Although Isabel is attentive to the individual needs of her students, her main focus as a teacher seems to be about promoting their ability to work together as a group to solve significant social issues. Although Isabel recognizes the importance of children working together to solve academic problems, she is more concerned about providing a context for them in which they can learn how to live together as a community. This perspective recognizes the differences that children bring to the classroom and how the group goes about living, working, and negotiating together. Isabel's practice focuses on the classroom as a collective of children, rather than on the individual children who make up the group.

Involved in the women's movement of the late 1960s, Isabel enters her classroom as a political activist, committed to gender equity. Her awareness of gender and feminist discourses informs her practice in several ways. For example, rather than observing children exclusively through a developmental lens and providing a developmentally appropriate curriculum, Isabel recognizes the significance of gender in children's daily lives and uses her authority and power as the teacher to create classroom structures that support a pedagogy intent on confronting gender bias. Isabel is aware that girls continue to lag in the physical sciences and are choosing math and science careers in disproportionately low numbers (AAUW, 1992), and therefore she makes certain that girls are encouraged and supported in their experiences with math and science in the classroom. This is evident when she instructs three girls to work together during center time to create patterns. Additionally, for work share, Isabel asks the "math team" to share their work with the entire class. When girls share, Isabel intervenes with appropriate comments, highlighting the successful ways in which they achieved their goals in the math context.

Isabel welcomed me into her classroom and made efforts to include me in the community of her kindergarten classroom and PS 99. After my first visit Isabel created a classroom folder with my name, and throughout the school year she filled it with district, school, and classroom notices, including valuable teacher resources. Brief, handwritten notes about critical gender incidents would appear, such as "Ask me about dramatic play" or "Take a look at the puppets on the door and ask me about them." Isabel also intentionally made my presence and research visible to others by introducing my project and me to parents and other teachers in the building, or by mentioning my research in her weekly newsletter. Isabel's interest in the investigation was demonstrated in her willingness to explore and question gender with me and with the children.

The Children

Purposeful sampling strategies were used to select children as focal points for my observations during the duration of the project. Isabel and I discussed a range of children who might potentially be information-rich cases. Using the logic behind intensity sampling (Patton, 1990), we were interested in focusing on children that we considered to be excellent, but not extreme or unusual, examples of cases that manifested the phenomenon of gender. We felt that these cases would allow us to better comprehend how children use their understandings of heterosexual discourses to regulate the gendered social order of the classroom. Therefore, Isabel and I spent time attempting to figure out which children explicitly displayed characteristics of hegemonic masculinity or emphasized femininity and who was involved in maintaining or resisting the gendered social order of the classroom. As a result of our conversations regarding possible focal students, my time and observations evolved, and I concentrated on the children we discussed collaboratively.

As a result of certain classroom events and discussions with Isabel, my observations often focused on the actions and talk of Alan, Anne, Breanna, James, Katy, Liza, Madison, and Theresa. I had not initially considered focusing on Anne, but conversations with Isabel made me think differently about Anne's gender experiences in the classroom. I tended to see Anne as a quiet and compliant Hispanic girl, who rarely spoke or raised her hand in class. Subsequently, I didn't consider her that interesting for the purposes of the project, and I found myself rarely sitting and talking with her during center time. Isabel, on the other hand, often brought up classroom events that involved Anne and the ways in which the intersection of gender, race, class, and sexuality might be influencing Anne's position in the classroom. Isabel's observations of and comments about Anne caused me to rethink my observational strategies and question the stance I had adopted. That is, I started to question my own values and beliefs about what I was considering important and relevant data. I became aware of which particular children appeared in my field notes and which ones were missing. A quick, informal quantitative analysis showed that certain children were getting noticed and some were not. More importantly, I began questioning why I was noticing some children more than others. After realizing that I was losing sight of children who were experiencing their school day from the margins of the classroom, possibly because of their gendered, racialized, classed, and sexualized identities, I began refocusing my observations on the children who had previously failed to make it into my field notes.

I agreed with Isabel that Anne would be an important case study because her gender experiences would highlight the intersection of gender, race, class, and sexuality. Throughout my time in the field, then, I consciously attempted to focus on Anne's talk and actions. In spite of these efforts, I found that after I had spent approximately 30 minutes in the classroom, Anne would disappear from my sight, and I would find myself focusing my attention and observations on other students in the classroom. After realizing this, I took a more purposeful approach toward collecting data about Anne. For example, before walking into the classroom I would remind myself that my observations would focus on Anne and I attempted to shadow Anne one morning during center time. Unfortunately, this strategy failed and I did not collect enough data to construct an in-depth case study of how Anne experienced gender in the classroom. I believed that this research story, especially my own subjectivity during the research process, was important and began documenting it through field notes.

While revisiting my collected data, I became cognizant of several missing voices. That is, I had little data on several of the girls and boys in the class. Although I found this interesting, it made me feel uncomfortable. I began raising several questions about my bias:

- Were the voices and actions of children such as Penny, Liam, and Charmaine not as prevalent in the collected texts because I was biased?
- How might my gender, race, class, and sexuality be influencing data collection?
- If gender is a social construction, then what about my research relationships with children? Aren't they gendered?

As a result of these questions, I chose to include a child whose experiences in the classroom were captured through field notes, audio and video data, and collected artifacts, but whose talk and actions were not as obvious, marked, or visible when compared to other children. Therefore, Penny, a quiet, working-class Asian American girl, was selected as one of the cases to explore for this book.

From the beginning of this study, Isabel and I discussed the possibility of creating a case study of Madison. Isabel suggested Madison because "she challenges and explores the boundaries of gender." While rereading the data sets, I was reminded of Madison's abilities to live with gender contradictions, confront gender norms, and bravely create counterdiscourses to access in the classroom. I knew she would be a fascinating, interesting, and important child to include as a case study, especially for questioning the assumed naturalness of gender.

The third child selected was Alan. Originally, I did not intend to include any cases of boys. As a feminist researcher, I felt inclined to focus exclusively on the girls and how they were experiencing and constructing gender in the classroom. However, feminist poststructuralism asserts that gender is a relation, created between males and females. Therefore, I decided it was necessary to analyze the relationships between boys and girls, specifically between hegemonic masculinity and other forms of gender. As a result, Alan was chosen because he is explicitly, distinctly, and unmistakably male. Supporting this decision, Isabel thoughtfully reminded me of the potentials for discovering new insights about gender from Alan and his maleness.

Throughout the process of constructing these three case studies, I was conscious of my responsibility to represent the gender discourses in the classroom, including the discourses that the children were involved in and accessed (Alldred, 1998; Ribbens & Edwards, 1998; Glesne & Peshkin, 1992; Jayaratne & Stewart, 1995; Lather, 1995). Throughout this book, children are not made out to be "cute"; instead their talk, play, and writings are presented as serious, complex, and important gender work. It must also be recognized that throughout data analysis and while constructing and reconstructing these three case studies, deliberate choices were made about which pieces of data to include or exclude in order to highlight discourses of heterosexuality and how Penny, Madison, and Alan did gender in their classroom.

A Self-Reflexive Research Design

The conceptual framework of feminist poststructuralism informed the research design and data collection methods and has relevance to the process of interrogating classroom research by teachers and researchers today. Current feminist analyses of traditional research methods have analyzed and reconceptualized the relationship between feminist researchers and those they collaborate with in research (Nielson, 1990; Ribbens & Edwards, 1998; Roberts, 1981; Stanley & Wise, 1993). Roman and Apple (1990) assert that feminist research must move beyond arguing the validity of women's subjectivities and toward recognizing the transformative potential of critical inquiries. They claim that recognizing power relationships between the researcher and researched is essential to understanding how social understandings are constituted in and through the research process. For this project this meant that I engaged myself with the research process in order to understand why some girls were marginalized in the classroom and society. Therefore, doing feminist research means not just taking a female's perspective, but also includes engaging in the research process to provide understandings that enable women and girls to transform their own world and become conscious of oppression. In other words, theory, praxis, and method become inseparable within feminist research (Fay, 1987; Nielson, 1990).

There is not a single feminist, poststructural, or feminist poststructuralist "method" of doing research. Rather, as a methodology, feminist poststructuralism draws from a variety of postpositivist paradigms of inquiry, each offering a different approach to generating and legitimating knowledge, but where the focus remains on the constructed rather than found worlds of knowledge. Using a feminist poststructuralist research design, the social, cultural, historical, and political construction of gender is placed at the center of the inquiry (Lather, 1992).

As praxis-oriented work or an act of consciousness-raising, this study was designed to turn critical thought into social action and as such has special and important relevance to the work of teachers and researchers who want to systematically interrogate and scrutinize their practices. This way of teaching and researching attempts to disrupt children's existing practices. For example, instead of going into the classroom and researching *on* or *about* children, this inquiry is about researching *with* them. Additionally, researching *with* children provides opportunities to intervene or disrupt inequitable power relations that exist. Some of the methods that were used to influence change in part of Isabel's practices as a teacher, researcher, and teacher educator, in children's actions as boys and girls, and in my pedagogies as a researcher and teacher educator included making time for extensive critical dialogue and questions. The methods used create the potential for challenging gender norms and improving the lives of girls and boys (Cook & Fonow, 1990; Fine, 1994; Lather, 1991; Nielson, 1990). Therefore, the time I spent as a researcher in the classroom included not only observing and documenting children's play and talk through field notes, audiotapes, and video recordings, but also developing relationships with Isabel and the children in which we were continuously uncovering and discovering the complexities of how the practices and discourses of heterosexuality operated within the context of the classroom. Questioning my beliefs, values, and practices did not stop here; subsequent chapters will integrate discussions of how this process continued over the course of my time in the classroom.

Reciprocity

According to Lather (1991), incorporating reciprocity in the research design is one way to create a project that empowers both the researcher and researched, as well as encourages consciousness-raising and transformation. Reciprocity occurred between myself as a researcher and those I was researching with in varying degrees and forms in the classroom. Although I am the main author and creator of this inquiry, an overarching goal was my attempt to restructure the often oppressive and inequitable relationships that exist between the researcher and the researched in many research projects (Alldred, 1998; Burman, 1992; Lather, 1991). Instead of a unidirectional process in which the researcher goes into the classroom to extract information and data from or about the research subjects, I used methods aimed at encouraging a more dialogical process or relationship between myself and those I was researching with. As a result, meanings about gender were negotiated with Isabel and the children through question posing, data collection, and analysis (Gitlin & Russell, 1994; Lather, 1991; Wilkinson, 1986).

Research Talks

Reciprocity is important in this context since it attempts to redefine the relationships I had with Isabel and the children, making change possible. It was built into the design in three ways. First, informal, reflective teacher interviews were conducted. These interviews varied and included discussions between Isabel and myself about the most effective data collection methods to use, how to distinguish certain children to observe and interview, and the process of identifying current classroom events worth investigating further. These reflective, ongoing conversations were originally planned to occur through scheduled monthly meetings. However, what actually transpired is more accurately described as informal, ongoing, and continuous "research talks." Every time I entered the classroom, I had some form of research talk with Isabel.

Research talks occurred daily and in a variety of ways. Sometimes they happened while walking up and down three flights of stairs when escorting the class to science, art, or music, during center time while children were playing, or in the classroom during lunch or after school. Although some of our research talks were short and quite informal, the information exchanged between us was always relevant from my perspective. Often these research talks influenced the entire research process and project. Since gender events and issues occurred daily in the classroom, it was both more practical and necessary to talk about them with Isabel as they happened, rather than wait to discuss them during monthly reflective interviews. Our daily research talks and collaborations were usually about immediate issues, and they made the research process attentive to the daily interactions and happenings in classroom life. These talks strengthened and maintained our collaborative relationship throughout the duration of the project.

Reflective Interviews

A second way that reciprocity was incorporated into the project was through monthly, scheduled, reflective interviews with selected children, which involved them analyzing episodes of video data. Here too, however, the immediate and continuous emergence of gender events and issues in the classroom encouraged informal talks with children on a daily basis. Reflective interviews or discussions with children would happen as a result of data being collected and reflected upon with Isabel during our research talks. Students were also asked to analyze data and were selected as a result of the gender events that occurred in the classroom and in conversations I had with Isabel. Each month a few selected students viewed and analyzed video data; the selection of these children was done collaboratively with Isabel, and was influenced by whether they were a part of the video data.

Sharing Data

A third and final way that we included reciprocity in the design of the investigation was by sharing data with the entire class. Isabel encouraged me to do this by taking part in either show-and-tell or work share sessions. In doing so, I had the opportunity to share my research, work, and initial findings with the class, as well as obtain and document children's analysis and interpretations of the data. Drawing from Gallas's work with sharing time (Gallas, 1994), Isabel held show-and-tell daily. Children signed up for show-and-tell, and on their day to share, they placed their show-and-tell item on a special block, sat in the large blue chair, and explained the item. Then they would ask the class, "Any questions or comments?" which was followed by a large class discussion conducted by the sharing child.

As an example of how reciprocity worked in this study, Isabel collected and saved children's self-portraits done during an art class, with the intention of sharing them with me because of their gendered themes. After looking through the self-portraits with Isabel during lunch, we talked about them and jointly raised several questions. We thought that it was interesting how a range of femininities, such as long hair, makeup, earrings, and hair ribbons, was represented in the artwork. We noticed how Valerie's collage of herself included her long hair literally flowing off the page, and how an Asian American girl named Kim, who has long dark hair and dark eyes, represented herself with blond hair, huge red lips, and blue eyes. Isabel thought it would be interesting to talk with the children about these self-portraits. Later that morning during center time, I sat with Valerie and Kim discussing their self-portraits. Then, during work share, Isabel chose to highlight the research and work that the three of us were engaged in during center time. Subsequently, Valerie, Kim, and I shared our conversations with the class, disclosing their views about the importance of looking and being beautiful.

Collecting Information on Gender in the Classroom

Data were obtained through the following sources: (1) field notes from observations of children playing and talking, (2) audio recordings of children playing and talking, (3) video recordings of children's talk and actions, (4) teacher interviews, (5) student interviews, and (6) student artifacts. The study spanned nine months and used both informal and formal techniques of research to establish relationships with the school and classroom community for collecting data.

One full day and two mornings a week were spent in the classroom as a participant observer. Going to the classroom three mornings a week allowed for opportunities to observe children making their entrance into the classroom, taking part in morning meeting and center time, and transitioning between morning activities. One of these mornings was spent videotaping children playing in the dramatic play center. I also usually spent time at another learning center talking with children and audio recording our conversations. Depending on classroom events or where focal students were playing, I would sometimes set up the video camera at the table toy center or one of the sand tables. On the days I was there only for the morning, when children went to music, art, or physical education I stayed in the classroom to conduct formal and informal reflective interviews with Isabel. When I spent the full day in the classroom, I accompanied the class to music, art, physical education, lunch, and recess, and I also took part in the afternoon routines of work share, writing workshop, and show-and-tell.

My Role as the Researcher

By the end of this study, children knew that my role in the classroom was that of a researcher. When children asked about my study or what I was writing down in my notebook, I responded truthfully. For instance, one day the children were sitting on the rug listening to Sue read a book. I was seated on the low tables behind them. James was seated next to Laura. He kept leaning toward her, making kissing noises into her ear. Laura was smiling and seemed to enjoy this. James was looking around the room and noticed me. He stopped and asked, "What are you writing?" I told him that I was making a note that he was making kissing noises in Laura's ear while Sue was reading her book. With a smile, James replied, "Oh," and turned back around. Approximately fifteen minutes later the class was in line, walking up three flights of stairs to Ta-Da. I happened to be at the end of the line. James and Laura were partners and were walking in front of me. James turned around and asked, "Why do you write down everything that kids say?" I told him that I think what kids say is important; especially what kindergartners have to say. I then told James that I wrote everything down in my notebook so that I wouldn't forget.

When asked what her concerns were about having me in the classroom, Isabel's response revealed how she was conscious of my role in the classroom and how she believed that students understood my role as a researcher too. For example:

> I don't want you to be absorbed into the community in a way that would make it difficult for you to do your research. And because the children are so accustomed to welcoming people and bringing them in, it's a concern of mine that that doesn't happen with you and this is a costly thing that you are doing in your life. I'm aware of the time and the financial stuff that goes into it and I want it to be valuable to you. And yet you're here and I know that they understand that you're here. It seems that they understand that you are here in a different way.

Children were aware of my desire to document their talk and actions. Breanna seemed to have a good sense of my goals as a researcher. For example, when the class was at physical education and I quietly walked into the gym and sat on top of the large blue mats, Breanna noticed me with a smile and wave, whispering, "I think you'll get some good stuff here."

My role as a participant observer fluctuated and changed throughout the research process. I also shifted uneasily between the position of passive observer and active participant, constantly reflecting on my role and the purpose of my work. At the beginning of this study, I was uncertain about the "appropriate" role I was to take during center time. As a relatively new researcher, I was not quite sure if asking children questions about what I was observing in the classroom was appropriate. I still had the image of a researcher as being a distant, objective, and impartial scientist. During one of our informal conversations at lunch, I discussed with Isabel a gender event I had observed in the classroom, and she said, "Mindy, ask him [James] about it! It would be interesting to know why he thinks that way and why he is drawing pictures like that. Just ask him!" Another time, Isabel told me, "Mindy, go ahead, be provocative! That's why you're here." I needed these nudges from Isabel and found that my role as an interventionist was slowly developing. As Isabel purposely brought gender issues into the discourse of the classroom for children to talk about, and as she encouraged me to explore emerging gender issues with the children during center time, I began feeling more comfortable with my researcher role. The questions and conversations I had with children about gender were never out of context. Rather, they transpired through my interactions and relationships with them, as well as the observations both Isabel and I were making in the classroom. Again, the kind of research I was doing in the classroom and how I was developing relationships with the children was very different from traditional early childhood research, when research is usually done on or about children.

Ethical Issues

While researching in the classroom, I was mindful of the inequitable relationship that existed between the children and myself. I made sure that they knew they had the right not to participate in our discussions. I did this by always asking children for their permission to audiotape and videotape their play and work. On two occasions I was asked by children not to document their work. The first request was during cleanup time, when I noticed both Kim and Liza sitting at the dollhouse. I thought it would be interesting to document how they had set up the furniture and plastic figures inside the house. Therefore, I walked over and asked them if I could take a picture of the work they had done at the dollhouse. Kim turned around in her seat and politely said, "No." I responded by just saying, "Okay."

The second request came from James, when he asked me to turn off my tape recorder while we were talking. It was center time, and James and I were sitting on the floor discussing a self-portrait he had done in art class.

James: What's this (pointing to my tape recorder)?

Mindy: It's my tape recorder, so I can remember what you tell me.

James: Is it taping right now?

Mindy: Yes, I want to remember the important things that you tell me. Because what you have to say is really important. (After a moment) How does it make you feel when you can't go to Lego?

James: Sad. Can we turn it off (the tape recorder)?

Mindy: Do you want me to turn the tape recorder off?

James: No . . . Um, turn it off, please (pointing to the tape recorder).

Mindy: Okay. (I turn off the tape recorder)

Critical Discourse Analysis

The general analytic strategies employed for describing and analyzing the discourses of heterosexuality and how children used them to regulate the gendered social order of the classroom relied on the conceptual framework of feminist poststructuralism. Foucault (1972) recommends that data analysis operate on the level of discourse, and this begins by treating all data as discourse. In this instance, all transcripts (field notes, observations, audiotapes, videotapes, interviews) and collected artifacts were read and interpreted as texts (Gavey, 1997).

Initial data analysis was ongoing and done simultaneously with collecting data in the field, enabling me to focus, shape, and modify the study as it proceeded (Glesne & Peshkin, 1992). However, the more formal phase of analysis occurred after the school year was over and my work in the field was completed. All of the data collected were transcribed. The transcription symbols and how they are used throughout the book are found in the Appendix.

One way of working with discourse is through the use of critical discourse analysis as a tool for seeing how broader forms of discourse and power are manifested in everyday texts (Gavey, 1997; Hicks, 1995–96; Luke, 1995; MacNaughton, 1998). The particular form of discourse analysis that I employed was influenced by feminist poststructuralist ideas, stressing the thoroughly discursive and textual nature of gendered life (Gill, 1995). Since discourse analysis views discourse as constructive and as a social practice, I began by identifying critical gender incidents and then analyzing them as discourses of heterosexuality available to and used by the children. From a feminist poststructuralist viewpoint, identifying these discourses is vital in understanding how the power-knowledge regimes of heterosexuality providing children with subject positions to work produce, reproduce, or challenge straight discourses in their talk and actions with each other (Hollway, 1984; Walkerdine, 1986).

Feminist poststructuralism informed the critical discourse analysis in four ways. First, close attention was given to the social context of language and its relations to structures of power, such as heterosexuality. Second, all social texts were approached in their own right and viewed as action-oriented media, rather than as transparent information channels. Third, analysis involved a careful reading of texts, with awareness of discursive patterns of meanings, contradictions, and inconsistencies. It is an approach that identifies the ways people use language and action to constitute their own and others' subjectivities. These processes are related to the regulation of the gendered social order. Fourth, discourse analysis proceeded with the assumption that these processes are neither static nor fixed, but rather unstable, fragmented, and inconsistent (Gavey, 1997).

Interpretation(s)

The following chapters of this book disclose how I saw and understood gender discourses in an early childhood classroom from theoretical perspectives often not utilized in early childhood education. It is important to remember that this is just one of many ways that children's talk and actions can be interpreted. Each classroom scenario, description of a child, or transcription can and should be read and reread, interpreted and reinterpreted from multiple perspectives. Each reader will approach these stories with their own gendered, racialized, classed, and sexualized lenses. We will probably interpret the same play scenario in different and contradictory ways. I hope so. I also hope that this story generates new discussions about feminist poststructuralism, queer theory, gender, teaching, and learning in early childhood education.

3

UNCOVERING THE HETEROSEXUAL MATRIX

The purpose of this chapter is to show the ways in which feminist post-structuralism and queer theory provide useful techniques for interpreting how children can take an active part in constructing their gendered identities. In doing so, this chapter uncovers the heterosexual matrix in the early childhood classroom by showing how gender is created, taken up, and performed through five particular heterosexual discourses: wearing femininity, body movements, makeup, beauty, and fashion talk. These five gender discourses disclose how children "do" gender in the classroom and how they use their knowledge of these discourses to constitute themselves as girls and boys in a heterosexual world. This perspective assumes that by "playing it straight," children take up heterosexual discourses that continue to maintain inequitable gender relations. These gender discourses are just some of the many competing and contradictory discourses that children access as they struggle to define and redefine who they are as gendered beings (Alloway, 1995; Davies, 2003; MacNaughton, 1996, 1998; Weedon, 1997). These five gender discourses were chosen because of the unique ways in which they reveal some of the structures that make up the heterosexual matrix and how it works to sustain gender norms in the early childhood class-room.

Locating the heterosexual matrix in practice provides readers with the opportunity to engage with alternative theories, seeing how children *themselves* understand and do gender everyday in the classroom. Becoming aware of the heterosexual matrix does not just happen. Instead, it is a complex process requiring teachers to rethink their current understandings of gender and young children. This shift in thinking is hard and challenging, especially if one is accustomed to seeing children in only a single way and through a developmental perspective.

Revisiting Feminist Poststructuralism and Queer Theory

This chapter illustrates the ways in which my own thinking about gender has been transformed. The account begins with how I saw gender in the classroom through hegemonic masculinity and emphasized femininity. My observations seemed to be structured and guided by a differences framework. At first, explicit and different gendered actions of boys and girls took up most of my observations. Then, as I continued to read feminist poststructuralist literature and queer theory, my observations changed. What I was seeing and hearing in the classroom were not just grounded in this investigation. Instead, I had opportunities to link my observations with the literature I was reading and discuss my initial findings in a community of practice. Slowly, I started seeing children not as individual gendered boys and girls, but rather as boys and girls taking part in power relationships that were located in particular social contexts. These relationships are seen as sites in which gender is constructed, reconstructed, and at times contested. It thus becomes possible to gain a sense of the gender discourses circulating in the classroom and the ways in which children access and use them to become gendered. Before continuing, I will need to explain further some of the concepts that were introduced in Chapter 1, because they underlie this chapter and are helpful in understanding how the five gender discourses were identified.

Hegemony

In their efforts to understand and challenge existing power relations between males and females, queer theorists are interested in exploring heterosexuality as a form of sexism and social regulation (Connell, 1987; Warner, 1993). This perspective holds that every culture has hegemonic or morally dominant forms of genders and sexualities that are considered right or proper for women and men (Lorber, 1994). The concept of hegemony was developed by Gramsci (1971) and has become a tool for cultural analysis. Hegemony is the domination of one group over another, with the partial consent of the dominated group. Hegemony is a process that perpetuates the status quo and is inherent in the social construction of gender.

Hegemonic Masculinity

Drawing from Gramsci's (1971) conceptualization of hegemony, hegemonic masculinity is defined as the dominant form of masculinity within a given society. Hegemonic masculinity, as defined by Connell (1987, 1996), is the cultural expression of the dominant form of masculinity that governs and subordinates other patterns of femininity and masculinity. Many forms of masculinity exist, and hegemonic masculinity is but one of them. Arguably, the most important feature of hegemonic masculinity is heterosexuality, which shapes the structural order of gender relations (Connell, 1987). Hegemonic masculinity works hard at maintaining and institutionalizing men's dominance over women, and therefore hegemonic masculinity is always constructed in relation to other forms of masculinity and femininity, marginalizing all other gendered ways of being (Connell, 1987, 1995).

Hegemonic masculinity is not the male sex role, but rather a culture's ideal or fantasy of what a male should be. If we consider that the classroom is a culture, then the children can define hegemonic masculinity based on the ideals they have for what a boy should be. Since hegemonic masculinity is an ideal form of masculinity, it is impossible to achieve. In other words, no matter how much boys and men aspire to be this kind of person and no matter how hard they work at it—for example, through having "six-pack" abs, driving fast cars, or dressing in cool clothes—this form of masculinity will never be attained because it is an illusion or fiction.

Since the discourse of hegemonic masculinity is both public and stylized, it is easy to locate and to see how it functions in the classroom.

Media images of strong, muscular, athletic, and active men are just one example of how hegemonic masculinity is stylized and inserted into the public realm.

Although social science research on gender has shown that there are multiple definitions of femininity and masculinity in different cultures and historical periods (i.e., Connell, 1995; Hargreaves, 1967; Willis, 1977), these gender regimes exist in relationship to a culture's notion of hegemonic masculinity. Furthermore, although more than one kind of masculinity can be found within a cultural setting, hegemonic masculinity prevails, coercing society and thus young children to attain this type of "normal" and desirable way of being.

Emphasized Femininity

According to Connell's (1987) understandings of femininity and masculinity, there is no femininity in our present society that is hegemonic. Instead, there is a type of femininity called emphasized femininity, which is defined around compliance, subordination, and accommodating the interests and desires of men. Like hegemonic masculinity, emphasized femininity is a very public construction. One might assume that if there is such a thing as hegemonic masculinity, then hegemonic femininity must also exist. However, feminist literature and past historical studies regarding a feminine character (Irigaray, 1981; Klein, 1946) claim that there is no femininity that is hegemonic in the sense that the dominant form of masculinity is hegemonic among all genders, making it capable of marginalizing and regulating both masculinity and femininity (Connell, 1987). Instead, Connell (1987) outlines three degrees of emphasized femininity found within society.

The most explicit form of emphasized femininity is defined around subordination and compliance and is oriented to accommodating the interests and desires of men—particularly the hegemonic male. Often, females choose to wear makeup because males desire and are attracted to this. Being desirable and getting noticed by particular males gives females a sense of power. As a result, emphasized femininity is *always* constructed in relation to hegemonic masculinity.

A less obvious degree of emphasized femininity occurs when girls or women enact strategies aimed at resisting gender norms or femininities.

This happens when we see girls choosing to wear clothes that allow them to get messy or be physically active, rather than always looking pretty and being passive.

The third level of emphasized femininity is subtle and difficult to locate, and it is seen when females utilize a combination of contradictory strategies. These approaches to femininity include the use of resistance, compliance, and cooperation in order to defy gender norms. When girls choose to wear unfeminine clothes yet use their body in provocative ways in order to be noticed or desired by men, they are deploying several strategies to enact femininity.

"Hegemonic" and "emphasized" signify positions of cultural authority, not total dominance, and therefore allow other forms of femininities and masculinities to persist (Connell, 1996). By locating hegemonic masculinity and emphasized femininity in the early childhood classroom, it becomes possible to see how they maintain practices that institutionalize men's dominance over women, therefore sustaining the current gendered social order.

The Heterosexual Matrix

Both feminist poststructuralism and queer theory are helpful frameworks for problematizing gender. Not only do they view gender as a social and political construction, but they also help us see the complexities of gender. For example, the dominant forms of hegemonic masculinity and emphasized femininity are influenced by heterosexual discourses, which are defined as stereotypical gendered norms and expectations considered appropriately male and female, including society's expectations that males and females will fall in love with and sexually desire a member of the opposite sex.

As I noted in Chapter 1, this perspective views gender as a performance that is constituted through the heterosexual matrix (Butler, 1990). The heterosexual matrix is designed to keep gender in its place and sustains normative ways of being gendered. The heterosexual matrix functions to link hegemonic masculinity and emphasized femininity into a coherent gendered discourse, and the reward is finding love with the opposite sex. The concept of genderedness becomes meaningless in the absence of heterosexuality as an institution, which is considered the normal and "right" way to be either a girl or a boy. This understanding of gender assumes that heterosexuality functions to produce regulatory notions of femininity and masculinity, implying that heterosexism, prejudice by heterosexuals against homosexuals, is a form of sexism. As a type of sexism, heterosexuality is neither natural nor freely chosen, but is rather a political institution that disempowers women and other marginalized populations (Rich, 1980). As an institution, heterosexuality entails a hierarchical and inequitable relationship between men and women.

These critiques of heterosexism are attacks not on heterosexual practices, but on the discourses of heterosexuality and how they have become embedded in the foundations of our thoughts and accepted as unproblematic; subsequently manifesting and maintaining power over females and others, such as lesbians, gays, bisexuals, and other marginalized identities (Butler, 1990; Rich, 1980; Sedgwick, 1990). Failing to question and interrogate heterosexuality as a form of sexism leads to simplistic understandings of gender.

Uncovering Gender Discourses

Although several gender discourses are found within the kindergarten classroom, I have chosen to illustrate how children can actively do gender in the classroom. Framed within the heterosexual matrix are the five gender discourses mentioned above: wearing femininity, body movements, makeup, beauty, and fashion talk. Not only do these discourses highlight how gender resides within the context of the classroom, but they also illuminate the ways in which power works and how these discourses and the heterosexual matrix work together to keep gender in its place. Although these gender discourses focus primarily on femininities, they still show how gender is constructed in relationship to hegemonic masculinity. It is possible that femininities are more noticeable because of my own gender, the large number of girls and women in the classroom, or the all-pervasiveness of hegemonic masculinity. According to Connell (1987), hegemonic masculinity regulates other forms of masculinity within society, while allowing various forms of subordinated femininity to be performed. As a result, actual femininities in our society are more diverse than masculinities, allowing for a greater range of gender variations to exist among girls.

Because I was interested in finding out how emphasized femininity and hegemonic masculinity are understood by children, several questions guided my observations when I first entered the classroom:

- Will emphasized femininity and hegemonic masculinity be present in the classroom?
- If so, what might they look, sound, and feel like?
- Will they be easy to find?
- How might my femininity affect my ability to locate hegemonic masculinity and emphasized femininity?

Wearing Femininities

The most obvious and explicit ways in which children practice gender and identify themselves as either female or male begins with how they wear their gender and present themselves to others during the school day. I often recorded what the girls wore to school, but I discovered that I rarely documented what the boys wore. On one hand, this seems reasonable since girls do have more options in their choice of clothing compared to boys, who only wear shirts and either pants or shorts to school. On the other hand, my own femaleness influences what I notice because being a girl is my reality, it is the gendered life I live.

Although children take up femininity and masculinity in different ways, it appears that it is important for the majority of young children to get their gender "right" (Davies, 2003). Not only do these children correctly do gender through the clothing they wear (i.e., none of the boys chose to wear skirts or dresses to school), but girls' fashion choices show further subtleties in the different ways of being right. Two of the most observable forms of femininity displayed include what the children named as "girly girls" and "cool girls." Being a girly girl means wearing frilly, ruffly, and cute outfits, with matching shoes, tights, and barrettes or ribbons. Pink is a desirable color for this look. Maintaining this form of femininity is important and seems to take great effort. I often noticed girls checking their appearance in the full-length mirror and overheard them discussing how hard it was to stay clean, neat, and pretty throughout the school day. As a consequence, it did not surprise me when Holly, with both her hair and the front of her dress covered with glue, told Madison, "That center was gooey and messy. I got real messy. Don't go there, especially if you want your clothes to stay pretty."

Not unpredictably, and consistent with studies done in classrooms to determine if boys and girls experience the curriculum equally (AAUW, 1992; Sadker & Sadker, 1995), this girly-girl form of femininity often restricts girls from participating in a wide range of school activities. For example, if wearing a dress or skirt, most girls avoid swinging or hanging upside down on the monkey bars because their underwear would show. While the children were playing outside, I heard Katy exclaim, "Oh, drats! (In a growling voice) I shouldn't . . . have . . . worn . . . this . . . dress! (Stomping her feet in frustration) Now I can't play on the monkey bars!"

Being a girly girl also enforces particular ways that the girls sit on the rug during group times:

> During morning meeting one day, Sophie frantically waves her hands, attempting to get Laura's attention to inform her that her panties are showing. From across the circle, Sophie shows Laura how to pull her skirt over her legs and sit with her knees together so that no one can see her panties.

Clothes enforce a different set of rules for the girls, which necessitate very clear limits on their behavior. Boys, on the other hand, are never observed worrying about how their clothing prevents them from participating in activities or being a certain kind of boy while sitting and listening to stories on the rug.

Another form of femininity that I noticed in the classroom is sophisticated, mature, and "cool." The "cool-girl" look clashes with the girly-girl form of femininity. Cool girls achieve their look by wearing clothes considered to be the latest in fashion, such as bell-bottom pants, Spice Girl logos, baseball caps turned backward, and the color black. Cool girls do not seem like they belong in a kindergarten classroom, painting at the easel or building with blocks. Instead, they look as if they should be out at a nightclub dancing. Valerie, who works hard at being a cool girl, always wears sophisticated and sexy outfits. Her clothes are never childish or frilly. One of her favorite outfits includes leopard-print stretch pants and a low-cut matching top, accented with fake black fur on the cuffs of her sleeves. Her outfit is complete with black, Harley-Davidson-style boots, making her look more like an MTV star than a 6-year-old.

Valerie is playing it straight in that her clothing is chosen to appeal to masculine ideas of attractiveness. Through her clothing, Valerie is choosing very clearly to position herself within the heterosexual matrix, as a female who wants to be desired by males. Valerie is performing this form of femininity even though other dominant discourses would seek to position young children as innocent or asexual.

A book that Liza wrote during center time, *Things That I Like and Things That I Do*, brought me further into the world of cool girls, specifically what cools girls are, what they like, and what they do.

According to Liza, cool girls like participating in a variety of activities, such as swimming, watching videotapes, dressing up like a boy, going to parties, doing gymnastics, and going shopping. Being a cool girl is not about complacency. Instead, the things that cool girls like to do take place in the public realm, which is often associated with

FAGS TAT I LIC ABD	*Things That I Like and*
FAGS TAT I DO	*Things That I Do*
I SAWAM IN TA WIY	I swim in the Y.
I LIC TO WICH TAPS	I like to watch tapes.
I LIC TO BE LIC A BOY	I like to be like a boy
AND TASUP LIC A BOY	and dress up like a boy
AND LIC A COL GRL	and like a cool girl.
I LIC TO GOW TO PRTEYS	I like to go to parties.
I LIC TO DO JMASTACS	I like to do gymnastics.
I LIC TO GOOY TO TA GAP	I like to go to the Gap.
I LIC TO GO TO COL PLASS	I like to go to cool places.
I LIC TO MAC DIGS	I like to make things.
TAS BAC IS DATACATD TO MIY FAMLE	This book is dedicated to my family.

masculinity (Donovan, 1992; Flax, 1990). Liza's desire to "be like a boy and dress up like a boy" shows her awareness of the lack of power within the cool-girl discourse. The only way for Liza to access power is through hegemonic masculinity.

Curious about Liza's understandings of femininity, I had the following conversation with her about cool girls:

Mindy: What's a cool girl?

Liza: Well, I like to wear bell-bottoms sometimes . . . and I like to wear shirts that are cool sometimes . . . and shoes that are cool.

Mindy: Who is a cool girl in this class?

Liza: Valerie, Kim, me, Breanna, and Madison . . . and Theresa, Sophie.

Mindy: Who isn't a cool girl?

Liza: Holly, Charmaine, and Anne.

Mindy: Is Nancy a cool girl?

Liza: No.

Mindy: What about Loren [preservice teacher]?

Liza: Yes.

Mindy: Why do you like to go to the Gap?

Liza: It has cool clothes.

Mindy: Is that where you get your cool-girl clothes?

Liza: Yes, some but not all cool-girl clothes. And I like to go to cool places.

Mindy: Where are the cool places?

Liza: Toy stores and toy places . . . and costume places and cool Gap places.

Mindy: Is it easy or hard being a cool girl?

Liza: It is so:oo:oo hard and it takes time. You aren't born this way. You have to work at it.

The importance that fashion plays in being a cool girl is apparent throughout my conversation with Liza. Also, several classmates are identified as being cool girls, including Valerie. Hearing Valerie named as a cool girl is not surprising, considering her popularity throughout the school. Valerie is popular with her classmates and older girls in the school. Often I saw a group of third-grade girls poke their heads into the classroom to tell Valerie hello. I once overhead a group of them mention that Valerie was "pretty cool for a kindergartner." Valerie's clothes, gender performances, and the conversations I had with her peers about cool girls led me to believe that the form of femininity Valerie performs is the coolest and most desired form of emphasized femininity in this classroom.

It is interesting to note that the three girls (Charmaine, Anne, and Nancy) identified by Liza as not cool are African American and come from working-class families. Here, the intersections of social class, race, and gender become evident. The fact that these girls are working-class, which prevents them from being able to purchase the right, cool clothes from the Gap, combined with their race, makes it difficult for them to be perceived as cool girls. The hierarchical nature of femininities also becomes apparent, as one girl is considered the coolest, and others are not. This can be attributed to the discourse of hegemonic masculinity and its ability to subordinate all forms of femininity (Connell, 1987). To be a player in the heterosexual game, a girl needs to perform emphasized femininity, which in this classroom includes wearing particular fashion styles. However, even though Valerie does this quite well, she doesn't have power, just a reflection of power. As a fashion girl, she is still a part of the heterosexual matrix and is socially constructed as subordinate to hegemonic masculinity.

Body Movements

Femininities are not exclusively embodied through clothing styles. I also observed girls carefully orchestrating how others would see them through "posing," a concept Gallas (1998) uses and expands upon in a classroom-based inquiry conducted with her first- and second-grade class. According to Gallas, posing is an act in which students are "trying on" a specific gender persona or a strategy used to influence others.

How children move their bodies and arrange how others perceive them through body movements is the second gender discourse. After noticing the different femininities that girls portray through their fashion choices, it becomes easier to see the ways that the girls physically move their bodies and pose for others through twirling, sulking, slouching, and curtsying. Each of these body movements is performed in relation to hegemonic masculinity and reinforces emphasized femininity to varying degrees. While enacting these highly gendered body movements, the girls are actively taking part in constructing and reconstructing heterosexual gender norms for themselves and others. As mentioned earlier, hegemony, according to Gramsci (1971), always involves the partial consent of the dominated group. In the body movements that the girls perform, they willingly take on a sexualized role that diminishes their own power.

Twirling I observed girls twirl strands of their hair while sitting on the rug for morning meeting, reading aloud, or show-and-tell. Once the girls became conscious of being watched, the twirling became exaggerated, while they boldly smiled at whoever was watching them. I also noticed girls twirling their skirts while moving their hips in what I consider to be sexualized ways. These body movements became more conspicuous when girls had an audience, such as when sharing work or reading a story to the entire class.

> For work share one day, Isabel asks Nancy, Sophie, and Charmaine to share the pattern work they did during center time. The three girls stand up in front of the class, while Isabel holds up the large plastic mat that contains the red and yellow plastic discs they used to make their patterns. When it is Sophie's turn to share, she does not stand still and explain her pattern. Instead, she begins swinging her hips back and forth, twirling her hair, fluttering her eyelashes, and gazing up toward the ceiling. She starts talking about her pattern work in a quiet voice but then suddenly changes to a high-pitched, singsong voice as she explains, "W:e:ll . . . I . . . um . . . . . . did this (pointing to a pattern) . . . . . . and . . . . . . um . . . ya kn:o:w . . . it was hard."

The class seemed to respond to this gender performance with interest, as the whispering between children stopped and they shifted their bodies to face Sophie. As soon as Sophie realized that she was being watched, her gestures became more animated. That is, the twirling of her hair became exaggerated, she placed her free hand on her hip and started swinging her hips back and forth, and she gazed up toward the ceiling. This display of femininity downplayed the hard work she did making patterns by bringing attention to her physical features, such as her hair and body.

Sophie also performed forms of femininity while participating in Ta-Da, a weekly dramatic arts enrichment program that the entire class attends.

> The class is playing the game Family Portrait, in which a small group of children is asked to go up on the stage and dance to music. While the music is playing, Ta-Da leaders call out a type of family for children to enact (i.e., the Monster Family, the Animal Family, the Ballet Family, and so on). After a few minutes of dancing, the music is stopped, and the leaders yell, "Pose!" At this time the group "poses" for a family portrait. During this game, Sophie's gendered body movements are most explicit while dancing with the Rock-and-Roll Family. Boys are moving their bodies with large gestures, such as taking big steps or jerking their shoulders back and forth to the beat of the music. Some of the boys move across the stage with air guitars or became drummers in a band. I watch as Sophie transforms from the quiet girl in the back to the lead singer of the band. While singing into her pretend microphone and wildly dancing around the stage, she seems to become conscious of her audience and changes her performance. First, she begins making eye contact with some of her friends. She then stops, gazes across the stage, twirls her skirt, and slowly shakes her hips. Two boys, Keith and Alan, are sitting in the front, and they smile back at Sophie while clapping and cheering her on. Although most of those watching are clapping and cheering, Sophie responds to Keith and Alan's attention by moving directly in front of them in order to dance for them.

Like her gender performances during work share, this too shows how she used her body to create femininity specifically for a dominant male audience. Sophie's actions were not ignored, but rather were recognized and supported by the boys.

Sulking and Slouching Sulking and slouching are two other body movements that receive attention in the classroom. Quite often when children slouch, their friends and the adults in the classroom notice them.
The two girls most often seen slouching in the classroom are Nancy
and Charmaine, both African American. Isabel is aware of the intersections between the sulk and children's race, class, and gender:

> It's the slouch that gets you noticed, and I find it common with
> my African American girls. I've told Nancy that she can't do
> this, it's not the way to greet a person. There are also girls and
> boys who whine to get attention, but I more often see the slouch
> in my African American girls.

Sulking and slouching position girls as helpless. Although these
body movements may not be as explicit as twirling one's body, clothes,
or hair, they are intentional. Being the last one to sit on the rug after
cleanup, lagging behind in line, dragging one's feet, slumping one's
shoulders, and having a sad face are all part of the sulk. Nancy often
sulks in order to get noticed.

> As children arrive in the classroom from physical education one
> day, they quickly sit on the rug, anticipating center time. A few
> seconds later, Nancy is the last student to walk through the
> door. She is taking her time getting to the rug. She is walking
> very slowly, with her head inclined toward the floor and her eyes
> cast down. She cautiously sits down in the back of the classroom,
> close to Loren, the preservice teacher, not on the rug with the
> rest of her class. Loren gently touches her back and whispers for
> her to move up on the rug, and Nancy scoots forward. Valerie
> moves over to sit next to her and begins rubbing and patting her
> back.
>   Nancy also chooses not to participate during cleanup time
> and instead quietly sits on the rug, where she slowly becomes the
> center of attention. First, Sue notices Nancy, and she walks over
> and asks in a kind voice, "What's wrong, Nancy?" Instead of
> immediately answering, Nancy lowers her head and shoulders
> closer to the floor and twists her body away from Sue. Then
> Valerie comes over, also asking Nancy what is wrong while gen-
> tly rubbing her back. Nancy looks up, slowly shaking her head,
> while whispering, "Nothing." Next, James arrives and tries to

comfort Nancy by gently placing his hand on her shoulder. Quickly, though, his hand is pushed away by Sue, who snaps, "Move away!"

Although the slouch gets Nancy noticed by several classmates, who all appear genuinely concerned about their friend's well being, Sue is disturbed when James comes over to help. Pushing James away can be interpreted as Sue resisting James' empathy and sensitivity toward Nancy—inappropriate behavior for a boy to be displaying. On the other hand, since it is common for both girls and boys in this classroom to console their friends, it is likely that Sue wants to be recognized for showing kindness, rather than James.

This moment on the rug illuminates how Sue understands the rules that flow from the logic of the heterosexual matrix. James is not playing it straight. That is, he is not following the gender rules that say boys are not emotional and do not show their feelings. Girls do not desire boys who are like this. Instead, James exhibits characteristics that are almost always considered feminine, and Sue knows it. In fact, she's calling him on it.

Curtsying The third type of body movement I observed being performed by girls is the act of curtsying. I first noticed it when the class had completed a performance in Ta-Da. The leaders would clap while exclaiming, "Great job! Now, everybody take a bow!" Instead of taking a bow, Katy loudly resisted their request, shouting, "Hey, what about a curtsy?" I repeatedly watched Katy curtsy after any kind of public performance, and Breanna soon followed suit. By refusing to take a bow, these girls are choosing to perform a particular form of femininity, and their actions help maintain gender differences.

Makeup

The third gender discourse, makeup, was found in several places in the classroom. Not only were children talking, writing, and drawing about makeup, but they were also bringing it to school. Entire books were being written by the girls about makeup, complete with detailed drawings about the kinds of makeup available, how it is correctly applied, and how it is used to attract boys and men.

Thinking that this might be an interesting gender topic, Isabel saved two books about makeup and put them in my folder. The following makeup book was written by Liza:

MKP	*Makeup*
ME WATHG MKP	Me wearing makeup.
LPSTK IS FOR LPS	Lipstick is for lips.
MSER IS FOR YR YIS	Mascara is for your eyes.
IY SATO IS FOR YR YIS	Eye shadow is for your eyes.
NAL PLAS US FOR YR NALS	Nail polish is for your nails.
BLS IS FOR YOR HEK	Blush is for your cheeks.
ME WATHG MKP	Me wearing the makeup.
LP LINR IS FOR YR LPS	Lip liner is for your lips.
PRFUM IS FOR YR BHY	Perfume is for your body.
CREM IS FOR YR BITY	Cream is for your body.
MKR CREM IS FOR BFOR	Makeup cream is for before
YR POT ON MKP	you put on makeup.

Since I found this book interesting and wanted to know more about it, I asked Liza if she could read her book out loud and then answer a few questions about makeup.

Mindy: Do you wear makeup?

Liza: Yeah.

Mindy: Do you ever wear makeup to school?

Liza: No. But I wear nail polish. See? (shows me her pink painted nails)

Mindy: Yes, you do. And nail polish is a type of makeup?

Liza: Yeah.

Mindy: So makeup just isn't for your face.

Liza: No.

Mindy: Who else wears makeup?

Liza: Theresa, Penny . . . sometimes they wear nail polish, and Kim sometimes wears nail polish, and Sophie.

Mindy:	Who doesn't wear makeup?
Liza:	Amy, Laura, and some other people like Sophie. I don't really think that she wears nail polish, but she might. And Amy, Laura, and maybe Sophie, and Holly she doesn't wear nail polish, but I think she might and she might not, but I think she does.
Mindy:	Well, why do you think girls choose to wear makeup?
Liza:	Because they like the style.
Mindy:	What does that mean?
Liza:	Well, when girls like to look beautiful.
Mindy:	Wow (pointing to a drawing of a girl wearing makeup), you even remembered to put on lip liner. Do you think that boys like girls who wear makeup?
Liza:	Yeah.
Mindy:	Do you think that's why girls wear makeup?
Liza:	No. (Conversation abruptly ends, as Liza is called to go out in the hall to finish a painting)

Liza wrote several books about makeup, each showing her knowledge of the cosmetic culture. This discussion with Liza also reveals her understandings of the politics of makeup—that is, when makeup can be worn by children (at home or while playing dress-up), what kinds of real makeup are allowed in the classroom (nail polish), who does and does not wear nail polish to school, and why some girls and women wear makeup. Liza's understandings about the difference between real and pretend makeup is quite different from those of the older children in upper elementary school that Thorne (1995) studied, who were still ambiguous about the different kinds of makeup. I wonder if this shows evidence of how gender discourses change over time and between social contexts. Although Liza believes that boys like girls who wear makeup, at the same time she does not think it is the only reason why girls choose to wear makeup. My conversation ended too quickly with Liza, as she was asked to go out into the hall to finish a painting. If I had the chance to finish this conversation, I would ask Liza why she thought that girls liked wearing makeup, how putting makeup on makes her feel, and if there are times when girls might not want to wear makeup.

Theresa, whose stories, drawings, and play often centered on the Disney character Ariel, understood makeup as a powerful tool for determining and expressing femininity. Theresa explained her drawing of the mermaid, Ariel: "This is Ariel. See? (Pointing to her mermaid drawing) She has lipstick and is showing off her stomach. She also has long hair, see? (Pointing to hair) Oh, and Ariel also has fingernail polish on."

It was important that I noticed Ariel's makeup (lipstick and nail polish), bare stomach, and long hair. For Theresa, Ariel is a beautiful object, someone who uses her accentuated feminine qualities to attract Prince Eric. Later that week, Theresa told me that she likes wearing red lipstick too, because it makes her pretty, adding, "Well, Ariel also likes to, no she **needs** to wear lipstick because Prince Eric likes it . . . a lot."

The discourse of makeup did not remain hidden within the realm of the girls' world. Instead, it made its way into the classroom curriculum when Liza brought an assortment of real and pretend makeup for her show-and-tell. In this classroom, as I noted previously, show-and-tell was a regular part of the daily routine. Drawing from the work of Gallas (1994), Isabel created show-and-tell as a space for children to take control over their learning and believes that it has the potential to support children's efforts at struggling with and confronting gender issues.

Show-and-tell happened daily, with children signing up for it in advance on a large calendar. Each child had a designated day when they would share. Show-and-tell began by first having children prepare the rug. This meant that the rug was cleared of materials and toys, and a large wooden block is placed in the middle of the rug and then covered with a special piece of fabric. Not only did the block help children to focus on the object being shared, but the object had to also fit on the block. After placing the show-and-tell item(s) on the block, the sharing child would then sit in Isabel's chairdescribing their item to the class. Then the sharing child would begin the large group discussion by asking, "Any questions or observations?" During this time, Isabel sits with the class, while the sharing child remained seated in Isabel's blue chair, fielding questions from the class. Although Isabel sometimes used her power as the teacher to intervene during show-and-tell, she usually did not make comments unlesss she was called a by the sharing child.

The following series of events occurred during show-and-tell and demonstrates how this common early childhood practice provides children opportunities to reinforce and resist the discourses of heterosexuality, which are embedded within the politics of makeup.

It is Liza's day for show-and-tell, and she has brought both real and pretend makeup to share with the class. Liza places a small stuffed animal, two bottles of pink nail polish, and a small purse on the block. She turns and walks to the large chair. She then sits and waits for the class to be quiet before beginning. The video camera is positioned so that Liza, who is sitting in the teacher's chair, is the main focus. On her left sit Nancy and Holly, and on her right sit Keith, Cheng, Katy, and Amy. Cheng's hand is raised, and Keith is leaning over him, whispering into his ear. Katy turns, looks at Cheng and Keith, and says, "Shhh! Be quiet."

Isabel: Okay, Liza, you can start.

Liza: I got the purse for Hanukkah, my mommy got it for me and the doll, I got it at a birthday party and I got that (stands up and points to the nail polish) from a kit, the lipstick from a kit, and the bracelet from my friend. Loren (calling on her, ignoring Cheng's raised hand).

Loren: Do you like to put the makeup on?

Liza: (Quietly and looking away) *I don't really put makeup on.* Katy (calling on her, still ignoring Cheng's raised hand).

Katy: Um, um, where did you get the bracelet from?

Liza: From Mexico. (Cheng's hand is raised and Keith is leaning toward him, whispering in his ear and trying to get his attention.) Kim.

Kim: Will you show us what's in the purse?

Liza gets up from the chair and walks to the block. She opens up the plastic purse and brings the purse back to the chair, where she begins taking small plastic items out of the purse and placing them in her lap. Keith is thumping Cheng's arm with his fingers. Cheng now sits up on his knees, to get a better look at the plastic items in Liza's lap.

Class: Wow! Look at that! (Girls to her left are up on their knees, leaning forward, and trying to get a closer look. Cheng leans his body forward, also trying to get a better look.)

Katy: Liza, do you think you can put the things on top of the block?

Liza: No. (Slowly gets up and places the makeup and other items from the purse on the block) Okay, there.

Cheng: (As Liza places the items on the block, Cheng names each of them out loud) Credit cards . . . keys . . . . . . comb . . . scissors . . . tickets . . . key chain . . . money . . . I love the purse too! . . . . . . .Pictures . . . lipstick. (Cheng leans toward Katy to tell her something. Looking straight ahead at Liza, Katy shoves Cheng with her elbow and then quickly raises her hand. She whispers to Cheng, "Stop," and then takes her hand and pushes him back to a seated position on the floor. Cheng raises his hand. Liza returns to her chair.)

Liza: Katy (ignoring Cheng's raised hand).

Katy: Um, I got the same purse and the makeup thing.

Liza: Which makeup thing? (Gets up from the chair and kneels next to the block.)

Katy: (Scoots forward and points to the makeup bag.) What are these scissors for?

Liza: Your toenails.

Sue: //Is the//

Katy: //I wasn't finished.

Sue: Um, is the makeup real?

Liza: (Kneeling at the block) These makeups are real (moving the fingernail polishes) just these.

Sue: Is there a special time when your mom lets you? Or (spoken very fast and softly) *can you put it on whenever you want?*

Liza: I really don't do it so much.

Sue: Does your mom sometimes tell you when you can put it on, or do you just sometimes do it?

Liza: Well, if my mom doesn't know then I don't tell her. Sue (ignoring Cheng's raised hand).

Sue: I don't have the same nail polishes, but I have the same pocket thing. And in my pocket thing it has a whole lot of different colored eye shadows, and I like it . . . a lot.

Liza: Thank you. Penny (ignoring Cheng's raised hand).

Penny: {inaudible}

Cheng: Will you turn around that? (Stands up and walks to the block, pointing to the nail polish. When Cheng returns to his seat and sits down, Keith shakes his head, with a disgusted look, and moves his body away from Cheng.)

Isabel: One more, Liza.

Liza: Valerie (ignoring Cheng's raised hand).

Valerie: Will you show us the eye shadow? Will you put them on?

Liza: (Gets up from the chair and moves the eye shadow kit to the front of the block, and begins to pick up the other items)

Cheng: I want to go to your playdate! (Pointing to the makeup) I want to see how everything works. Especially this! (Stands up and points to the eye shadow. Laughter from the class. Keith stares at Cheng and slowly shakes his head.)

This episode highlights how the discourse of makeup circulates in the classroom and how children use their knowledge of both the heterosexual matrix and makeup to maintain particular ways to be girls and boys. Some of the politics that children are aware of include the idea that makeup is only for women and the notion that it is not appropriate for young children to wear "real" makeup. Liza's responses indicate that she is not allowed yet to wear real makeup and that it is only for pretend play. Liza and Sue both know that makeup is taboo, as they share how they conceal makeup from adults. In fact, Liza shares that she follows the "don't ask, don't tell" policy with her mom. Valerie also daringly asks Liza if she will put the eye shadow on at school.

Throughout show-and-tell, Cheng's curiosity about girls' makeup is ignored and resisted by his peers in a variety of ways. First, Liza ignores him throughout show-and-tell and refuses to call on him. Did she choose not to call on Cheng because boys aren't supposed to be interested in makeup and she thought that he wouldn't have a "good" question, or was she afraid that he might make fun of what she brought? When Cheng finally makes a comment, he blurts it out, and Keith's reaction is unfavorable. Keith's body language and comments indicate that he does not approve of Cheng's interest in the makeup. While Cheng attempts to engage Katy in a quiet conversation on the rug, she ignores him and physically pushes him away. Finally, when Cheng excitedly shows an interest in the makeup, his classmates laugh at him. At this moment, Cheng and the entire class are learning powerfully that makeup is not for boys, but only for girls.

Ignoring Cheng's raised hand, pushing Cheng away, and laughing at Cheng's interest in the makeup are strategies used by the children to regulate gender. Davies (2003) refers to these strategies as category maintenance work, in which children are attempting to suppress Cheng's interest in the makeup and thereby support the assumption that boys should only be interested in masculine activities and should not want to learn more about makeup or desire to wear it. While some might argue that this particular show-and-tell provides the opportunity for femininity and articles associated with the feminine domain to be celebrated and valued within the curriculum, others might consider this show-and-tell as a practice that supports heteronormativity. The feminine articles that Liza brings from home, and in essence her culture, capture the interest of the girls and one boy. At the same time, this group of young children works hard at letting Cheng know that his interest in makeup is not "normal" for boys. By not allowing Cheng to venture into the feminine realm, or by making it difficult for him to do so, the children are actively regulating the gendered social order of their class and supporting the heterosexual matrix. The discourse about makeup, as seen in this vignette, illustrates clearly that young children know how to regulate gender. If children know how to marginalize particular forms of femininities and masculinities, they also have the ability to support them.

Beauty

The fourth gender discourse is about the idea of beauty. I realized the importance of beauty while talking with children about makeup, and saw how these discourses are interconnected and work together to support gender norms. When I asked a small group of girls about their interest in makeup and the books about makeup that some children were writing in class, I was repeatedly told how makeup was used by girls and women "to be more beautiful" and "to get boyfriends."

The value that a small group of girls placed on being beautiful and pretty became evident in the dramatic play area while they were pretending to be princesses. Davies' (2003) work with preschool children shows how the romantic mythology of princes and princesses is a story line that plays a powerful part in the construction of emphasized femininity and hegemonic masculinity. Often, early childhood teachers and parents view children's pretend play as "simply play," failing to recognize how gender is created and re-created in these storylines. As children enact the storylines of princes and princesses, the importance of being pretty and the role it plays in creating femininities and masculinities provide another opportunity for locating the heterosexual matrix in the classroom.

I often watched as girls pretended to be beautiful princesses attending extravagant parties and balls where they would meet and dance with a handsome prince. Dressing up in ball gowns and jewelry was a requirement for attending such social events. A variety of dress-up clothes such as party dresses, veils, scarves, high-heeled shoes, earrings, necklaces, bracelets, and handbags were available at the dramatic play center. The girls used these accessories to transform into beautiful dancing princesses.

"Getting ready" was a ritual enacted in the dramatic play center as girls pretended to get ready for their dates with older boyfriends and princes. One day I recorded Nancy, Katy, and Theresa spending 28 minutes, out of their 39-minute center time, "getting ready" for a wedding and honeymoon.

> Katy is putting on a shiny blue party dress, a pink veil, and jewelry. While getting dressed, she chats with Theresa and Nancy about her upcoming marriage. There is much talk about the importance of looking beautiful and pretty. Katy says, "I have to look so beautiful for my husband or else he won't want to marry me. Boys don't like you if you don't wear jewelry, makeup, and have long hair. That's why I need the dress and jewels." As Katy discusses the importance of being beautiful, she is trying on the dresses, scarves, and other accessories available at the learning center. Each time that she puts on a piece of jewelry, she stands back, posing for Nancy and Theresa, and asks, "How do I look?" While doing this, her voice begins to change, she twirls her hair, and she starts to swing her whole body back and forth. Theresa puts on the pink and black party dress, leaving nothing fancy for Nancy to wear.
>
> Both Theresa and Nancy begin tying scarves onto their ponytails, giving them long hair that they are able to toss and flip around. Although Katy has short hair, she manages to tie one of the scarves around her head, so that she also has long hair. Katy fluffs her hair with both of her hands and shakes her head. The girls frequently compliment each other's long hair, exclaiming, "Oh, your hair is so long and be::yoo::ti::ful!"
>
> Katy and Theresa begin packing for the honeymoon. Nancy picks up a plastic makeup compact and pretends to apply powder to her face.

Nancy: (Walking toward Katy) M:o:m, do you want to look beautiful and in style? (She begins applying powder to Katy's face.) Here, it really does make you more beautiful.

Katy: (Stops packing and allows Nancy to apply powder on her face). Oh, darling!

> After finishing with Katy's makeup, Nancy resumes powdering her own nose.

Theresa: (Looking at Katy.) Oh, you look beautiful! Are you wearing long hair to the wedding?

Katy: Yeah. (Takes her hand and strokes the scarf while moving her hips back and forth. She now takes off her dress and packs it.) Guys, we really have to look beautiful.

Theresa's scarf has fallen out of her hair and Nancy is tying it back on her ponytail. Katy continues to pack for their trip.

Katy: Nancy, guys, get in your seats//

Nancy: Wait a second, I'm helping her.

Katy: Come on guys, get in the car . . . We are leaving in five minutes.

Theresa: (Walking toward the car) Well, I have long hair.

Katy, Nancy, and Theresa spend more than half of their center time becoming beautiful. For these girls, beautiful is connected with "getting ready" as they try on party dresses and jewelry, put on makeup, and fix their hair. Their talk and actions show how important it is to look beautiful. As we saw earlier, emphasized femininity is about women constructing themselves according to male desires. Katy, Theresa, and Nancy understand this message, and their actions reinforce the heterosexual matrix.

Being pretty and beautiful were not just characteristics important in the dramatic play area; both adults and children were seen recognizing and praising particular forms of femininity. Adults were sometimes heard saying, "Oh, doesn't that dress look beautiful! You look so pretty today!" As Sue and Valerie entered the science classroom, the science teacher noticed and greeted them with, "My, you both are so dressed up and **pretty**! It looks as though you are both going to a party." Children also took an active role in complimenting each other's outfits, especially how particular barrettes and bracelets made them look "oh so beautiful!" Interestingly, boys were never heard complimenting girls on their clothes or appearances.

These everyday and seemingly innocent comments become concerns if we think about the importance of language and how it constructs gender. For example, praising particular gendered categories, such as "pretty" and "beautiful," creates and sustains the gendered elements of the current social structure, as such praise values certain ways of being a girl while ignoring and marginalizing other ways of being gendered (Davies, 2003). As we will see later, when girls do not wear beautiful things, they can become marginalized by their peers or ignored by adults.

By praising and acknowledging certain forms of femininity, both adults and children reinforce and strengthen the heterosexual matrix. As the school year progressed and my understandings of the messages conveyed though these comments deepened, I found myself cringing when adults remarked on girls' physical appearance. Nonetheless, such cultural positioning is deeply ingrained. Despite seeing and acknowledging this practice, I found myself participating anyway when I exclaimed, "Oh, Mary, you look so pretty in that dress? Is it new?"

Fashion Talk

Fashion talk is the fifth gender discourse and includes how children talk about desirable forms of femininity and masculinity, which in this classroom were embodied through "fashion girls" and "fashion guys." Fashion talk disclosed that fashion girls and fashion guys were not constituted in the same ways. For example, fashion girls were defined first by how they dressed and then second by their actions, particularly how they behaved toward others. Fashion guys, on the other hand, were determined almost exclusively by their physical actions. Through fashion talk, I discovered that not everyone was considered to be a fashion girl or a fashion guy. The following exchange shows how children defined and named fashion girls and fashion guys in their classroom. Subsequently, I will explore the idea of fashion girls and fashion guys, showing how these embody normative understandings of gender. By exploring the performativity of fashion girls and fashion guys, it became apparent that some children were resisting these "proper"—and, some might say, limiting—ways of being either a girl or a boy.

I first heard the term "fashion girls" used by Alan while we were sorting Lego action figures by their gender. When discussing with Alan which Lego action figures were girls and which ones were boys, he kept comparing the girl Lego action figures with the fashion girls in his class. When I asked Alan to explain what he meant by fashion girls, he replied, "W:e:ll, first they wear cool clothes . . . and they have to wear makeup and perfume. Fashion girls aren't interested in being police because they **like** sitting around and being beautiful. And, oh yeah, **all** fashion girls have boyfriends." I found Alan's comments interesting and wrote in my research journal, "Alan said something quite provocative today. It had to do with this idea of fashion girls and they had boyfriends. Is this evidence of the heterosexual matrix?"

The following day, Alan initiated a conversation about fashion girls, telling me whom he considered to be the fashion girls and fashion boys in his class. Soon more children joined us at the snack table, and the following discussion transpired:

Mindy: Charmaine, who do you think are the top three fashion girls?

Charmaine: Me, Kim, Liza, Debbie.

.

.

.

Alan: ///Valerie . . . Breanna . . . Katy . . .

Mindy: Who are the top three fashion guys?

Charmaine: Alan//

Alan: //I'm the king of boys (pointing to himself).

Ian: I know (shrugging).

Charmaine: Alan, Liam . . . . . . (having trouble naming a third) Raoul//

Alan: //Me, Majindra, Ian

Mindy: Why are they fashion boys?

Alan: Because they always play.

Mindy: Oh, so it has nothing to do with what they wear?

Alan: *But I'm the king,* (loudly) I'm the king of boys, so I know who the fashion boys are.

Mindy: So if you're the king of the boys, who's the queen of the girls?

Charmaine: Me.

Alan: **No.** Valerie. Valerie's the top fashion girl. But I'm the top boy of fashion. Number one, number one (making the number one with his finger).

From this conversation, certain children are named as either fashion girls or fashion guys, with emphasis placed by Alan on Valerie being the most fashionable. This comment implies a hierarchy that exists within femininity, raising questions about which femininities and masculinities are most valued and by whom. However, as this conversation shows, Charmaine has a different idea, one that competes with Alan's, about who is the queen of the girls. Whose point of view is valued here—that of Alan, the dominant, white, middle-class male, or that of Charmaine, the submissive, African American, working-class girl?

Another interesting aspect of this discussion is how Alan wields his power as a boy by interrupting others and raising his voice in order to have his ideas heard. Unfortunately, as these audio recordings show, I failed to recognize Alan's talk and actions as hegemonic masculinity and did not use my power as the adult researcher to intervene and hear from the other children at the table. Not surprisingly, Alan continues dominating the fashion talk at the art table.

Mindy: Alan, what does it mean to be fashionable?

Alan: Fashion, it means . . . *sexy* (whispering while lowering his head and eyes).

Mindy: It means what?

Alan: It means *very sexy* (looking at me with a smile on his face).

Mindy: So there are some fashion girls in this classroom?

Alan: Mmm-hmmm (looks away and down at the floor).

Mindy: And who do you think is the number-one fashion girl?

Alan: (Looking straight at me) Valerie.

According to Alan, fashionable means sexy. By whispering, lowering his head and eyes, looking away, and then smiling at me, Alan indicates that he is aware that this subject is taboo. His words and actions show his desire to imagine the heterosexual possibilities between girls and boys. It is as though Alan has moved beyond the safe discourse of what fashion girls and guys wear and toward an understanding of what they might get up to.

Fashion Girls This particular occurrence of fashion talk encouraged me to find out more about the ways in which the children understood femininity and masculinity. Interested in hearing other children's perspectives about fashion girls, I set out to talk with Katy and Liza, two girls who were often identified as fashion girls by their peers.

> It is center time, and Liza and Katy are working at reading on the rug. They are lying on the floor, decorating a large birthday message for their friend Valerie. Hundreds of crayons are spread out on the floor, and they are deciding how they will decorate the card and write a birthday message. I join them and help color the birthday message. While decorating the card, we talked about what it means to be a fashion girl.

Mindy: I have a question for you two. A few weeks ago Alan told me that there are girls in the classroom who are considered fashion girls. Do you know what that means?

Liza: Yeah.

Katy: Yeah. It means that they're beautiful.

Mindy: Do you have to dress a certain way . . . to be a fashion girl?

Katy: Yes.

Mindy: Who would you say are the fashion girls in this classroom?

Katy: Valerie, Breanna, Debbie, Liza, and me.

Liza: And Penny.

Katy: Debbie and Sue.

Mindy: Would Madison be a fashion girl?

Liza: No, she always wears jeans and things like that.

Katy: Well, Theresa is not **really** a fashion girl. She always
            wears like pants and shirts and not really dresses. Some-
            times I wear dresses.

Mindy: In order to be a fashion girl do you have to wear dresses?

Katy: Yes. Wait, well, actually you can be a fashion girl and not
            wear a dress. See, Liza is a fashion girl and she isn't wear-
            ing a dress. But um, Theresa wears things that don't add
            up. Like she wears a green shirt and purple pants. These
            (pointing to her outfit) add up. **Because** this is blue
            (pointing to her top) and this is purple (pointing to her
            pants). They go together.

Liza and Katy show that being a fashion girl is not just about being a
cultural icon, but about having a sense of style or knowledge about how
accessories, clothing, and colors go together to create a fashion-girl
look. In this classroom, there are certain girls who Katy and Liza consider to be fashionable. Again, Valerie's name came up as an example of
a fashion girl. Because of Valerie's race and class, she has access to the
discourses of power and privilege, allowing her to adopt a particular
feminine style, which Davies (2003) calls high-status femininity.

As our conversation continues, it becomes evident that girls do not
really have the luxury of being either a girly girl or a cool girl. There is
no choice, because as we shall see, all of the fashion girls are cool girls.

Mindy: Are there lots of fashion girls in this classroom?

Debbie: Yes//

Breanna: //Laura, Amy, and Sophie//

Debbie: //And all the girls can't be fashion girls.

Mindy: They can't? Is there one girl that wouldn't be a fashion
            girl?

Breanna: Liza//

Debbie: //and Breanna. You know why? (Looking over at
            Breanna) Because she hit me in the mouth going down
            the stairs.

Mindy: So a fashion girl is more than just what you wear?

Debbie: Yeah.

Breanna: She has to **be** a certain way.

Debbie: Good and nice.

Breanna: And be very beautiful.

Although beauty is seen as an important characteristic for fashion girls, particular behaviors are also expected from them. These comments reveal the complexities of what it means to be a fashion girl. Additionally, Laura and Amy, twins who are from the Czech Republic and do not speak English, are named as fashion girls. This conversation shows how different girls have different understandings of these discourses, indicating that knowledge about fashion girls can be contested. That is, several discourses about fashion girls become visible, and each of these discourses can compete with the others to become definitive. These discourses are influenced by several factors, such as the social context and the girls involved. It would be easy to hope that Laura and Amy represent an example of girls accessing power outside of the dominant discourse of being white, middle class, and English speaking. However, I would argue that because of the intersections of race, class, gender, and other factors, they still remain within the heterosexual matrix. Both their attractiveness (both girls had long blond hair) and their inability to communicate (which made them quiet) reinforced emphasized femininity; thus they remained within the heterosexual matrix.

As the conversation proceeded, Debbie and Breanna continued explaining their conceptualizations of fashion girls.

Debbie: And you know what? Some fashion girls are **so:oo:oo**
            beautiful that they're jealous.

Mindy: Really? What are they jealous of? . . . . . . Are you jealous
            of fashion girls?

Debbie: No.

Breanna: I'm very fashionable but I'm not jealous.

Debbie: Me too.

Mindy: So, do you have to work at being fashionable?

Breanna: Yeah. It's hard work.

Debbie: And you know what? They can't do anything mean to anybody. That's fashionable.

Mindy: Are there certain ways that a fashion girl would act?

Debbie: Yes . . . they . . .

Breanna: Some mean girls say, *"You're **so:oo:oo** perfect, you're **so:oo:oo** perfect you get all you want."* (Tone and pitch of voice change, with her voice becoming highly animated. Begins to move her shoulders back and forth and twirl hair.)

Mindy: Do girls say that to other girls in this classroom?

Debbie: (Nodding) Mmm-hmmm. Breanna says that to me.

Mindy: Do fashion girls have boyfriends?

Breanna: I do.

Debbie: I have two. Another person that's not in my class . . . and he's 7.

.

.

.

Debbie: *Breanna . . . Breanna . . . you're too perfect.* (Tone and pitch of voice change, while she moves shoulders back and forth.)

Breanna: But ladies, ladies are perfect. They can't eat off of the floor. You know why? . . . They will get sick . . . and not be beautiful.

Mindy: Do fashion girls have good manners?

Breanna: Yes (nodding).

Debbie: Oh yes (nodding).

Mindy: Are fashion girls smart?

Breanna: Yes

Debbie: (Nods)

Being a fashion girl is complicated and hard work. Not only are fashion girls beautiful, nice, polite, and smart, but they are sometimes jealous of other girls. Breanna and Debbie both feel that fashion girls are desirable to boys and often have boyfriends. Debbie's comment about having two boyfriends, with one being older, implies that power and prestige are gained by having more and older boyfriends. Age has now surfaced as another dimension of identity.

Fashion talk with these children never included same-sex desire. That is, girls were never overheard dreaming about and romanticizing falling in love with other girls, and boys never talked about kissing boys. The power of the heterosexual matrix is such that same-sex desire remains highly invisible for all age groups. Therefore it is no surprise that these possibilities remain unspoken by the children in this class.

It is interesting how the girly girls are not recognized by their peers as fashion girls. I believe that the girly girls are playing it safe with the clothes they choose to wear to school. For example, by wearing particular clothes that do not emphasize their sexuality, they do not risk becoming entangled within the heterosexual matrix and are not recognized by their peers as such.

Analyzing children's talk and actions about fashion girls makes visible the discourses of heterosexuality. It uncovers how these discourses work to normalize and maintain the current gendered social order of the classroom. Furthermore, these children are observed using their understandings of gender norms to regulate the gendered social order and construct themselves as gendered beings within the heterosexual matrix.

Fashion Guys As with emphasized femininity in the previous section, discourses of hegemonic masculinity are expressed through children's talk about fashion guys. As children conversed with me and each other about fashion guys, it became possible to see how hegemonic masculinity regulates and marginalizes other types of masculinities and femininities. As a result, all other forms of gender are constructed through and in relation to hegemonic masculinity (Connell, 1987).

The following conversation with Alan reveals how fashion boys are understood:

Mindy: Can both girls and boys be fashionable?

Alan: Boys can't.

Mindy: But you told me that you were the king of fashion?

Alan: Hmmm, king? . . . Oh. Fashion boys can fight. **No, no** (moving both arms back and forth), fashion boys **do action movies!**

Mindy: Who would be the number-one fashion boy in this class-room?

Alan: Actually, nobody in this classroom. Somebody that is already grown up. Pierce {Brosnan}.

Mindy: Pierce who?

Alan: Pierce {Brosnan}! He is a movie star . . . He plays James Bond and he bungee-jumps.

Mindy: So he's a fashion guy?

Alan: Yeah, he, he has, he breaks through glass and shoots people!

Mindy: Do you want to be like that?

Alan: Yeah.

Alan's knowledge about fashion guys is similar to the characteristics of hegemonic masculinity described by Connell (1987, 1996). For Alan, fashion guys were older men, Hollywood movie stars, who are trying to achieve an ideal form of masculinity. During this conversation, the importance of what a fashion guy wears is not mentioned as an important attribute of this form of masculinity. Instead, Alan appreciates and values the physical and violent actions of James Bond.

Interested in what other children thought, I asked Ian, Breanna, and Debbie some questions about fashion boys. As the following conversation shows, they too have a clear sense of how the heterosexual matrix and hegemonic masculinity regulates femininity.

Mindy: Do you know what a fashion boy is? (Looking at and addressing Breanna)

Ian: I know what a fashion boy is, except I never saw one.

Mindy: Well, Alan said he saw one. So if a fashion girl has to be nice, do fashion boys also need to be nice?

Breanna: A fashion girl **has** to marry a fashion boy.

Ian: I'm not a boy. I'm a scientist.

Debbie: (Showing me her new pierced ears and earrings) Look at my ears.

Mindy: Could a fashion boy marry an un-fashion girl or a girl who is not considered a fashion girl?

Debbie: Nuh-uh (shaking head). No way!

Breanna: Nuh-uh (shaking head).

Mindy: Why not?

Debbie: Because fashion boys like fashion girls better than not fashion girls.

Mindy: So if you want to get married, do you need to be a fashion girl?

Debbie: (Nods)

Mindy: Can anyone be a fashion girl?

Debbie: No ... well ... maybe.

During this discussion I attempted to find out if the behaviors associated with fashion girls are similar to fashion boy behaviors. Although I never got an answer, I did find out from Breanna that fashion girls have to marry fashion boys. By emphasizing the word *has*, Breanna understands that there are no other real choices for fashion girls and boys. Her knowledge of the discourse of heterosexuality illuminates how girls are constructed in relation to hegemonic masculinity and how this construction of gender relies on the heterosexual matrix to exist.

Attempting to explore children's understandings of the heterosexual matrix further, I inquired about the possibility of fashion boys and girls marrying unfashionable girls and boys. Debbie and Breanna both firmly agree that this is impossible. The reward for being a fashion girl is "getting" the fashion boy and living "happily ever after." For Debbie, being a fashion girl is a desirable form of femininity to perform in relation to and for fashion boys. Furthermore, Debbie's final response is an example of how girls often struggle to perform emphasized femininity. That is, by changing her response and agreeing with me, Debbie performs the nice and "good" student.

This conversation tells us much more than just how hegemonic masculinity is resisted in the classroom. It also illuminates the ways in which gender is resisted and desired by children. Ian renounces his gender, labeling himself as an androgynous scientist. Although hegemonic masculinity is actively reinforcing gender norms, Ian chooses not to be a part of it. Ian's responses show his awareness of fashion guys and what they signify, substantiating the idea that while fashion boys do not exist in real life, they embody ideals and norms that boys are constantly attempting to achieve. If I had recognized Ian's declaration of not being a boy as a form of resistance, could I have supported his desires in the classroom? For Ian, hegemonic masculinity is hard work, and he might not be willing to play this game. Or perhaps hegemonic masculinity provides too few options for Ian and he is trying to create different forms of masculinity to access.

Throughout my time in the classroom, it was evident that children had a clear sense of hegemonic masculinity, emphasized femininity, and how these worked to position females and males relationally within the heterosexual matrix. In the following conversation with Katy and Liza, we are able to see how they desire, rather than resist, inserting themselves into the discourse of emphasized femininity.

Mindy: Are there any fashion guys in kindergarten?

Katy: Yes. Cheng wore a suit yesterday.

Mindy: But that was just once. Would you consider Cheng to be a fashion boy?

Liza: Well . . .

Katy: Not really.

Mindy: Who would be considered a fashion boy in this class?

Katy: Alan. Do you know what he says to me? Once he tried to
           kiss me on the lips.

Mindy: Oh, he did? What did you do?

Katy: I kept my hands in my lap . . . but he kept kissing me.

Mindy: Did anyone find out?

Katy: No. *Anyway, I hate him.* (Quickly said, while shaking
           her head)

Mindy: You do? Why?

Katy: W:e:ll (smiling and scrunching her shoulders up), he is a
           little nice.

Although Katy initially associates clothing with being a fashion guy,
she soon realizes that this might not solely determine hegemonic masculinity. When both girls are directly asked if Cheng is a fashion boy,
Liza hesitates and Katy quickly says no. Instead, Alan is named as a
fashion boy. Cheng's interest in makeup, as seen earlier during Liza's
show-and-tell, makes it clear to others that he does not understand the
gender rules and is therefore not powerful. Or perhaps Cheng is choosing not to embody hegemonic masculinity because he likes things associated with femininity.

Interestingly, Katy's reasons for naming Alan as a fashion guy are
similar to Alan's basis for naming Valerie a fashion girl (see page 82).
That is, both Katy and Alan understand how the relational aspect of
the heterosexual matrix is based on desire. Katy supports the heterosexual matrix and wants to be a part of it. Instead of resisting particular
forms of femininity, she placidly sits, keeping her hands in her lap,
while waiting to be kissed. This gender performance is an example of
how Katy is playing it straight, as she chooses to act in ways that Alan
will find desirable. Even if Katy really doesn't like Alan, she knows and
wants the status and prestige that come with performing particular
forms of femininity. At the end of our conversation, Katy's talk and
actions show the gender contradictions she faces and works through in
her every day life. It is clear that these young children know this discourse well, both desiring and resisting becoming a part of the heterosexual matrix.

Shifting the Gaze

These examples illustrate some ways in which kindergartners know and understand the heterosexual game and are playing it straight in the classroom. The games that they play are shaped by a variety of gender discourses, but these discourses are in turn shaped by the children, as they negotiate their play together. By using alternative perspectives to understand children's engagement with gender, it became possible to untangle some of the threads of the heterosexual matrix.

However, this is only part of the story. How do individual children experience being a girl or a boy in this early childhood classroom? Now our gaze will shift across the gender terrain, as the next three chapters focus on Alan, Madison, and Penny and how each does gender in unique ways. Most teachers will recognize these children and their experiences will sound familiar. Perhaps these three case studies will provoke teachers to undertake new ways of understanding children's conversations and play. Instead of assuming that the children's behaviors are determined by biology or a result of being socialized, perhaps teachers will open themselves to seeing these children as active agents in the world of gender, moving towards creating new pedagogies that will support and challenge gender in the early childhood classroom.

4

ALAN: POWER BROKER

"No way! Boys are not allowed to play with Barbies."

Building on the gender discourses presented previously, this chapter shows how power is a dimension of gender and how one boy uses power to construct his gender identity and the identities of others in the classroom. Like the work that Davies (2003) has done with young children, showing how hegemonic masculinity is a dominant and powerful form that some boys work hard to achieve, this chapter introduces Alan, the ways that he values masculine discourses, and how he uses them to regulate gender in the classroom. The ways that gender influences teaching and researching relationships will also be explored, revealing how all relationships are gendered. Finally, I discuss how a small group of girls and Isabel confront Alan's beliefs about gender.

Alan and His "Boyhood"

At the beginning of this project, Alan was five years old. He is an Anglo-American boy and part of a stable and caring middle-class family, including his mother, father, and older brother, Franklin. Both his mother and father work full time outside the home, and Alan and Franklin are cared for by their babysitter, Rose. Alan has a special relationship with Rose, which became clear when I watched the two of them greet each other in the afternoons with smiles and hugs, share special jokes with each other, and leave the school building holding hands.

Alan's family is important to him, and he often talks and writes about them at school. For instance, conversations initiated by Alan often begin with "Guess what my brother did last night?" "Guess what my baby sitter did this morning?" or "Guess what my father got me from his trip?" When Alan talks about his older brother, Franklin, it is with respect and admiration. Franklin often pops his head into the classroom to either say hi to Alan or quickly advise Alan which items he should share for show-and-tell. One day for show-and-tell, Alan insisted that Franklin's expertise was needed for explaining to the class the facts regarding his trip to the Baseball Hall of Fame and his baseball trading card collection. Alan declared, "I **need** to talk to Franklin. I need to know the **facts**. It's important that I get it right."

Alan writes stories, books, and poems about his family and dedicates them to his family members. In the newspaper he co-wrote with Ian, Alan featured a story about a special family trip to Disneyland that he took with his mother and brother. In the following poem, published in the class poetry book *Poetry Every Day, Poetry Every Way*, Alan writes about the excitement of waiting for his dad at the airport:

At the Airport

We went to wait for Daddy.

Mommy had Starbucks coffee.

And then Daddy came out.

We held up our poster.

It said, "WELCOME HOME DADDY!"

Adults often draw on the dominant discourses of gender, such as those mentioned in Chapter 1, to explain children's talk, actions, and relations with others in the classroom. Isabel did this when explaining some of Alan's actions in the classroom. For instance, one day while talking about how children embody gender in the classroom, she stated, "Alan is gendered before ever entering the classroom. He is so like his dad. Once you meet Alan's dad, you understand Alan and how he is." A feminist poststructuralist perspective makes room for a different explanation of Alan's talk and actions as a performance that he actively constructs. The following field notes show Alan displaying highly gendered actions that Isabel imagines Alan's father doing at home during Passover:

> Children are called by Loren individually to find a seat and then wait for the haroseth that was made during center time to be served for snack. When Alan is chosen, he quickly finds an empty table, sits at the "head" of the table, and spreads both his arms out and grabs the sides of the table, saying loudly, "This is *my* group . . . I'm in charge!"

A socialization perspective of gender sees Alan modeling what he observes his father doing at home. But, his father would never say this, so it is not just Alan copying what he hears at home. Instead, it is power mongering. Alan chooses to enact this form of masculinity because of the power that he is able to access as the male at this table.

Alan has dark brown eyes and hair, and wears his hair short. He most often wears tennis shoes, jeans, a T-shirt, and a baseball cap to school. He did, however, once come to school dressed formally, with a navy blue sport coat over his T-shirt. I remember this outfit because of the way in which he proudly displayed his jacket and himself. While sitting at a table writing field notes, I felt a tap on my shoulder. I turned around to find Alan standing with both of his arms stretched out, saying with a big grin, "What do you think?" I was a bit confused, so I asked, "Think about what?" Alan dramatically took a step back, pointed to his jacket, and with a smile replied, "This . . . look . . . I wanted to be dressed up." Like the fashion girls, Alan found power in his style of dress. Particular ways of dressing reinforce different forms of femininity and masculinity. For example, in some working-class male cultures, the mode of dress that is powerful is the white muscle T-shirt, gold chain, and large tattoo. Alan's middle-class male culture values a different kind of fashion. Alan is aware of these rules, and by wearing the sport jacket, he is attempting to position himself in relation to the females in the classroom. This sort of dress will make others have different feelings toward Alan. However, since Alan was not seen wearing the sport coat again, it did not have the desired effect that he wished or did not give him access to enough power.

Alan likes engaging in heteronormative discourses. He enjoys school and his favorite part of the school day is "going to the park and chasing girls." During center time, he does not seem to have one favorite learning center. Instead of choosing a center based on the activity found there, Alan's decisions are influenced by who is working at each learning center. When called on to choose a learning center, Alan rises to his knees and looks around the classroom before carefully deciding where he is going to play. More often than not, Alan is found sitting next to a female adult, rather than one of his classmates, during center time.

Most early childhood teachers would enjoy having Alan in their class. He is articulate and independent, and he knows how to listen and follow rules. Not only does Alan follow the classroom rules, he is also excellent at enforcing them. If Isabel tells a child who is sharing during show-and-tell that he or she may take only two more questions from the class, Alan ensures that the rule is followed, making certain that no more than two questions are asked. Because the rules of the heterosexual matrix give Alan much of his power, perhaps he has an interest in enforcing them.

Disregarding Femininity

Alan disregards and shows little interest in femininity. Talking about dolls, the color pink, or Barbie evokes a cringe, rolling of the eyes, and groans of disappointment from him. While waiting for work share to begin one day, Isabel carefully placed children's drawings and constructions, completed at the paper work table during center time, in the middle of the rug. Kelly's complex three-dimensional house created out of construction paper and Theresa's drawings of the mermaid Ariel were chosen for work share. As Theresa began explaining her drawing, Alan groaned loudly, interrupting her as he complained, "She's talking about the Little Mermaid **again**." While saying this, Alan rolled his eyes and turned his body away from Theresa, showing everyone that he neither was interested in nor valued the work that Theresa did during center time. Emphasizing his disinterest, he continued to turn his body farther and farther away from Theresa as she talked about her drawing.

Another time when Isabel discussed with the entire class the possibility of boys not being able to go to the table toy center to play with Lego because a group of girls had made a week-long reservation to play there, Alan slowly shook his head every time Isabel mentioned Lego work done by the girls. Finally, when Isabel described the girls' Lego work as being "hot stuff," Alan closed his eyes and placed both hands on his head while loudly moaning, "Ohhhh no!"

Regulating Gender

Alan seems to accept that boys and girls are different and uses this "factual" knowledge to regulate gender relationships in the classroom. Davies (2003) calls this "category-maintenance work" (p. 31), and it occurs when children ensure that gender differences are maintained in the classroom. For Alan, there are certain and distinct ways to be *either* a girl *or* a boy, with not much room for the blurring of these two genders. It is not uncommon to hear Alan loudly and confidently state to a group of friends that boys neither play with Barbie dolls nor like the color pink. For Alan, it simply is not a possibility. While playing Lego with a small group of boys, he explained with certainty, "Look . . . boys are supposed to do boy things and girls, well, they do all those girly things. That is how it is! Boys play football, girls are cheerleaders . . . **and** we aren't going to mess with it. That is final!"

By accepting gender in terms of differences and valuing particular ways of being a boy, Alan regulates gender in this classroom. These understandings about hegemonic masculinity emerge most noticeably with Alan through fashion talk. Alan's knowledge of hegemonic masculinity also situates him as an expert with the boys in the classroom, and they often turn to him for advice regarding gender issues. For example, Cheng was observed consulting Alan about whether a certain piece of colored construction paper was a girl or boy color before deciding whether or not to use it. This was particularly interesting, given Cheng's continuing negotiations about how he would like to be positioned in the classroom as a boy. Or, as children were opening their Valentine's Day cards, Ian turned to show Alan one of his cards, asking, "Hey, is this a girl or a boy Valentine?" In these instances Alan is positioned as knowledgeable and powerful among the boys in his class.

Valuing Hegemonic Masculinity

Alan's beliefs about gender differences also influence the value he places on characteristics often associated with dominant forms of masculinity, such as the importance of visible work, having an idea first, and working independently, and how he uses these to gain power in the classroom.

Alan appreciates visible work, and it is important for him that others recognize his ideas and efforts. The significance that Alan places on how he is perceived by others coincides with Davies' (1994) descriptions of the privileged male speaker as not only having certainty about who he is but also placing a high value on attaching work and ideas to his individual self. One afternoon during writing workshop I observed the significance for Alan of being recognized for having an idea first.

> The class is seated on the rug and they are brainstorming ideas to include in good-bye cards they will be making for Hazel, a preservice teacher who will be completing her field placement. Isabel is seated in front of the group in her blue chair, while Loren (another preservice teacher) and I are seated in chairs behind the children.

Isabel: Does anyone have any ideas about what you could write on Hazel's good-bye card?

Alan: I'll miss you.

James: I love you.

Liza: I wish you could stay.

Breanna: I wish you could stay more often.

Sue: I wish you could stay so you could do more murals.

Cheng: I like you.

Keith: I like you and I like that you play with me.

Loren: We will miss you.

Alan: (Turns around toward Loren with a puzzled look, while pointing to himself) Hey, **I** said that first . . . that's what I said.

Although some teachers might see Alan as a caring and thoughtful boy who has developed a relationship with his preservice teacher, others might also see the gender discourses at play through the importance that Alan places on being recognized for *his* ideas. Instead of simply accepting Loren's contribution, Alan physically turns around defensively, drawing attention to his claim that what Loren said was really *his* idea and that he came up with it first. Another interesting point about this small group discussion is the way in which Loren chooses to add on to Alan's ideas, rather than to the suggestions of any of the other children in the group. This is an example of how teachers treat children differently, and in this case Loren is extending Alan's ideas rather than choosing to highlight someone else's contributions.

Isabel brought to my attention another way that Alan publicly reinforces the masculine sphere by distinguishing between *starting* an idea and *adding on* to an idea. Isabel first noticed this while the class was brainstorming their weekly Memory Web. On Fridays the class creates a Memory Web, which is part of the weekly newsletter sent home to families, conveying important events and accomplishments of the school week. Some examples taken from a Memory Web include "We learned a new baseball song," "Liam's mom and dad came to the park," or "Kelly did 299 jump ropes." Adding on to an idea begins with a child starting an idea by stating, for example, "Kim's mom came to the park with peeled, cut-up apples." Then Breanna adds on, "They were very juicy and very delicious and they were cut like moons," followed by Nancy's contribution, "Some people used toothpicks." According to Isabel, Alan distinguishes between these two ways of contributing to the Memory Web. He does this repeatedly by drawing attention to the two different ways of contributing when he states, "No, that was my idea and I thought of it first, not Katy. Besides, I gave it first, I didn't add on."

The importance of working independently rather than cooperatively is another characteristic often associated with hegemonic masculinity

(Davies, 1994; Kimmel, 1990). Again, the value that Alan places on *his* ideas and work is reinforced in several comments he makes in the classroom.

> While waiting for children to become engaged in classroom activities, I notice Ian and Alan working at the paper work table. Remembering that they have been co-creating a newspaper earlier in the week, I walk over to investigate. Without moving from his spot on the floor, Alan looks up from the table to explain, "Ian is writing and *I'm* (pointing to himself) doing all of the work!" A few minutes later, Alan finds me working with Charmaine. He interrupts us, pulling on my arm and saying, "Hey, look at this, Mindy. (Showing me the newspaper) *I* did all of the work. It's good."

These examples show the ways that Alan values visible work, having original ideas, and working independently. Alan values these particular ways of being because they make him feel important and give him more control than other ways of learning. These are central themes within the discourse of hegemonic masculinity. Alan's knowledge of his place within the heterosexual matrix means that females will pay attention to him. This knowledge also leads to him seeking me out and engaging me in a gendered relationship in which he expects to experience a sense of his own masculine power. My responses, more often than not, confirm his sense of self, while supporting the heterosexual matrix.

What Do the Girls Think?

Some of the girls were cognizant of Alan's desires and attempts to enact hegemonic masculinity. While talking with Sue about the types of books that some of her classmates would and would not write, we see how she understands Alan's masculinity.

> It is center time and I am at the hall table reading and talking with Sue. We have been reading and discussing books that children have written during writing workshop.

> Mindy:　(With Alan's books placed on the table) Alan wrote about his friend Majindra, sports, and this is a book about the

class. Do you think Alan would ever write a book about dolls?

Sue: No.

.

.

.

Mindy: Now what about the other boys? Would every boy in this class write about sports? Would James write about sports?

Sue: That's a tough one. Because it's really tough because we haven't asked him.

Mindy: But what do you think?

Sue: Maybe, he might.

Mindy: How about if we went through the boys in this class and predict if they would ever write a story about dolls. Would Raoul ever write a story about dolls?

Sue: No.

Mindy: Ian?

Sue: No . . . well maybe . . . I don't know.

Mindy: Liam?

Sue: No way.

Mindy: Majindra?

Sue: Maybe.

Mindy: Keith?

Sue: No . . . well, yes.

Mindy: Cheng?

Sue: No . . . he might want to, but he wouldn't.

Mindy: Alan?

Sue: **N::o::: way!** He would not. It is not a possibility. (Moving hands back and forth and shaking head)

Mindy: What about James again?

Sue: Probably not.

Mindy: I wonder if it would be worth asking everyone in class.

Sue: Maybe. We could do that if you want.

For Sue, it is highly unlikely (implied by her raised voice and dramatic arm movements) that Alan would ever write a book or story about feminized objects. However, she also understands that the boys in her class express a range of masculinities and interests, and some would consider writing about items that are often associated with femininity. Sue is also perceptive about Cheng's desire to write about dolls, but she realizes that he might find it, like the makeup, too risky a discourse to take up. However, Sue understands that Alan is a boy who chooses not to take up these marginal forms of masculinity. Instead, Alan wants to engage in heteronormative discourses.

I rarely saw Alan playing with the girls, and according to Sophie and Katy, they preferred not playing with him either. I asked Sophie and Katy if they liked the boys playing with them at the dramatic play center. After giggling, Katy explained, "Well, no . . . And definitely not Alan. He always wants to be bad." Sophie then added, "You know, he always wants us to have a cool-girl voice." When I asked what she meant by a cool-girl voice, Katy said, "You know, sexy and stuff." Katy and Sophie know that Alan desires them to play in a particular way, wanting them to perform femininities that support and work with hegemonic masculinity. The particular form of femininity that Alan wants the girls to embody fails to offer the prestige and power the girls want to experience. Katy and Sophie already know that at times talking in a sexy, cool-girl voice diminishes their power.

Sometimes Alan's actions are considered unfair by a few of the girls. Instead of ignoring Alan's actions or comments, these girls challenge his biases against girls. One day when it was Alan's turn for show-and-tell, Sue noticed that he didn't call on any of the girls. She exclaimed, "Hey! Alan, you didn't call on any girls!" Then Katy, looking around the circle and making eye contact with Madison, said, "Yeah, you're right. That's not fair." According to Isabel, the girls who are seen confronting Alan are those most comfortable pushing the boundaries of gender and living with the gender contradictions in today's society.

Seeing Is Believing?

As I walk into the classroom to begin preparing for another day of research, Isabel greets me by insisting that I quickly go downstairs and watch the class climb the rope in the gym. The urgency in her tone of voice indicates that I cannot miss this event. With notebook in hand, I race downstairs to watch these five- and six-year-olds climb a large rope that is hanging from the cafeteria ceiling. As one child attempts to climb the rope, the rest of the class watches while sitting on the floor along the perimeter of a big blue mat. I notice that several of the boys, such as Keith, Ian, Liam, and James, are unable to reach the top of the rope.

At first, it appears that as the children climb the rope they are being cheered on and encouraged by their classmates. However, I discover that the cheering is not the same for everyone. That is, when a girl fails to reach the ceiling and then slides down the rope, her friends console her with pats on the back while shaking their heads, coupled with comments such as "Good job," "Better luck next time," and "Oh, it's okay." However, when a boy is unable to reach the top of the rope and returns to the blue mat, he is ignored.

I note that when a girl is successful and touches the ceiling, it is only other girls cheering and giving congratulations, whereas the boys react with silence. As more girls experience success at climbing the rope, Keith loses interest in the activity. He stops watching the girls climb and attempts to engage in a conversation with the boys sitting around him.

Alan quietly and intensely watches as more girls successfully reach the top of the rope and touch the ceiling. The girls are consistently outperforming the boys, confronting his notion of how the world is and should be. As each girl touches the ceiling, Alan physically deflates. That is, his shoulders fall and he slumps toward the floor while looking away from the action. He seems bewildered by this scene, as he shakes his head in disbelief when Katie, Breanna, Sue, Penny, and Madison each climb the rope and touch the ceiling. Incidentally, Alan is one of only two boys who can climb to the top of the rope.

The reaction from the class seems to contradict research findings that consistently reveal males receiving more attention in schools than females (e.g., Brophy & Good, 1974; Ebbeck, 1984; Jones, 1989; Lockheed, 1984; Sadker & Sadker, 1986). In this case, the girls are receiving attention for their physical achievements and the boys are ignored. It is possible that the boys are overlooked because their inability to achieve this physical feat is not part of the dominant paradigm. It is as if the class cannot see a boy unsuccessfully climbing the rope; they ignore the fact that some boys are unable to accomplish this feat. For boys, it is shameful to publicly fail a physical challenge, and for his peers to notice his failure and respond would only deepen his humiliation.

It is worth noting that although the girls are receiving attention for their physical attempts and success, it is not coming from the boys. As a group, these boys are quietly but effectively resisting the notion that the girls are outperforming them physically.

Alan's view of this event is interesting. Instead of seeing the girls' feat as unbelievable, he is unable to acknowledge that the girls in his class are physically able. For most people, as with Alan, if we don't talk about it, we can believe it didn't happen. A few days later, I questioned Alan about the girls' ability to climb the rope.

Mindy: Who is the strongest in the class?

Alan: Oh, I'll tell you. (Sits down next to me on the floor) Raoul, Keith, James.

Mindy: Those are the three strongest boys?

Alan: Yeah.

Mindy: Who are the three strongest girls?

Alan: Nobody. (He is looking directly at me and his voice and facial expression indicate that I have asked a ridiculous question)

Mindy: None of the girls are strong?

Alan: (Turns away from me, shrugging)

Mindy: I saw some of those girls climbing that rope—they looked pretty strong.

Alan:	It was boys. Loren is strong.
Mindy:	Yeah. Loren is strong. But I also saw Breanna, Katy, and Penny climb the rope//
Alan:	{inaudible}. It was boys. Loren is strong.
Mindy:	That doesn't mean that they're strong?
Alan:	Nuh-huh. (Shakes head) If they're strong, they will have big, big, big muscles. (He bends his arm to show off his muscle, and tenses his entire body)
Mindy:	And they shouldn't have big muscles?
Alan:	No, they **don't**. I don't see any. (Stands up, turns away, and begins kicking the wall)

Alan's understandings about who is physically strong in his class show his determination to keep boys and girls different. Even though Alan and I both watched several girls in his class climb the rope during physical education, he is unable to consider any of the girls as strong. He aggressively resists these gender contradictions by dismissing my point of view when he interrupts me and by abruptly grabbing paper out of my hand. He also attempts to redirect the conversation to a topic that he wants to discuss. When I contradict Alan's beliefs about what the girls in his class can do, he struggles with being positioned as powerless, because for that moment in our conversation, girls are stronger and more powerful. Instead of talking about his feelings, Alan reacts in physical ways and performs hegemonic masculinity, presumably with the goal of ending our conversation.

Appealing to the Women

Rarely was Alan seen playing alone or with his female classmates. Instead, he was most often found either playing with some of the boys or laughing and talking with one of the female adults. He was popular with the female adults in the school, such as the preservice teachers, teaching assistants, or the cafeteria workers. I often wondered why these women were drawn to Alan. Was it his middle-class values, white skin, good looks, and intellectual competence? Or was it his ability to initiate and maintain lively conversations with most of the adults in the classroom?

Alan's Relationship With Loren

One of the most significant relationships that Alan had in the classroom was with one of the female preservice teachers, named Loren. Alan and Loren spent a considerable amount of time together, especially during center time. Isabel noticed this, mentioning that she often has preservice teachers who are drawn to one or two of the children. She believes that these relationships occur when preservice teachers see a part of themselves in particular children. On the other hand, I believe that these relationships are also influenced by the heterosexual matrix and that gendered power relationships do exist between children and adults.

> As part of her preservice teaching experience, Loren is responsible for creating a semester-long unit. For this requirement, she has chosen to integrate the curriculum around nutrition, planning a variety of cooking activities to do with the class. One of these activities is making popcorn to sell at an upcoming school-wide festival. For one week, Loren helps children prepare the popcorn bags during center time at the reading center on the rug. Alan knows that Loren will be working at this center for the entire week and is disappointed when it quickly fills up with children on Monday. During center time, while seated at the paper work table, Alan watches Loren and a small group of children prepare the popcorn bags. While pointing toward Loren, Alan says, "I want to be over there, with Loren." In order to ensure that he is able to work with Loren, Alan writes a note making a reservation at that learning center. As a result, Alan is able to go to the reading center the next day. Unfortunately, Loren does not stay for the duration of center time because she has a meeting to attend. After realizing that Loren will not be staying in the classroom for center time, Alan no longer wants to stay at the reading center on the rug. Instead, he wanders around the room, asking adults and classmates, "Where is Loren?" Walking past me at paper work, Alan grins, clenches his fists, and says, "Oh, I'm gonna kill that Loren! Where is she? She said that popcorn is on the rug! I have been waiting all week to be with her."

A close analysis of Loren and Alan's interactions reveals that their adult-child or teacher-student relationship is not neutral, but rather part of a gendered power relationship. Through their relationship, discourses of gender circulate, and both Loren and Alan are socially constructed through the heterosexual matrix.

> One day Isabel places a vegetable mural that children made during center time in the middle of the rug for work share. The mural shows the range of vegetables that children brought to include in the vegetable soup that the class will be making with Loren after reading the book Stone Soup (Brown, 1975). To begin work share, Isabel talks about each vegetable, emphasizing how children and their families contribute in a variety of ways in the making of the vegetable soup. Loren then begins sharing with the class how a small group of children (Alan, Charmaine, and Ian) helped chop vegetables during center time. Loren is immediately interrupted by Alan, who loudly states, "I did it all by myself! I did it all by myself!" Loren smiles at Alan, responding, "Yes, you did, Alan. You were such a good helper."

Although this classroom moment shows Alan valuing independent work, it also reveals the gendered relationship that exists between Alan and Loren. Both Alan and Loren are performing emphasized femininity and hegemonic masculinity in relationship to and for each other. Loren chooses to respond to Alan because of his maleness and feels good when Alan gives her attention. However, by positioning Alan as a "helper," Loren continues to hold onto some power as the teacher.

Another example of how Loren and Alan are situated within the heterosexual matrix can be seen when Loren was conducting a large group discussion about her nutrition unit. While sitting in the front of the class, Loren drew the food pyramid onto a large piece of chart paper and then asked children to help her fill it in.

Alan: **Ugh!** (slapping his hand on his knee) We have to do the food pyramid again? We do this with you every time. Why won't you give us something harder? Like words.

Loren: *W:e:ll, today I have a **new** idea for the food pyramid* (voice changes). We are going to do it a little differently (looking directly at Alan).

Alan: No more food pyramid! No more food pyramid! **No more food pyramid**! (He is chanting while also slapping his

knees with his hands. The chanting gets increasingly
louder.)

Loren: How about if we do it a little differently (looking at
            Alan)? *It's going to be a challenge* . . . (voice changes)
            Okay? Well, I'm going to be thinking about a food, and I
            will give you hints about it and then you have to guess
            what kind of food I am thinking of//

Alan: (Raises his hand quickly)

Loren: (Stops what she is saying, looks at Alan, and calls on him)
            //Is this a better way to do the food pyramid?

Alan: Yes.

Loren: Okay, Alan, you can go first.

Alan gains control of this lesson by telling Loren that the activity she
has planned is not interesting. He does this by reacting negatively to
Loren's idea and then strengthens it by chanting, "No more food pyramid!" Loren responds by changing her tone of voice, looking directly at
Alan, and then altering her idea to accommodate Alan's request. Alan is
using his gendered power, whether consciously or not, to situate Loren
within the heterosexual relationship. Some questions that this scene
raises include: Why does Alan respond in the way that he does? Why
don't the girls feel able to make similar demands? Why didn't Loren
choose to ignore Alan's behavior? Instead, she plays into his wishes by
presenting him with a challenge. Loren accommodates Alan's interrup-
tions and demands as she calls on him to answer a question that she put
forth to the entire class. In this episode, Loren is positioned as compliant and submissive in relation to the powerful male, Alan.

My "Objective" Research Relationship With Alan

Loren was not the only female adult located within the heterosexual
matrix. I found that I was part of this gender relationship too. Realizing
that I was involved in a gendered research relationship with Alan
was troubling. This discovery challenged me to question my role as a
feminist researcher and my own investment in heterosexist behaviors.
The following examples attempt to show how Alan and I are part of a
gendered power relationship and how we are positioned relationally

within and through the heterosexual matrix. Uncovering these gender discourses makes it possible to see how heteronormativity is pervasive in the research relationship I established with Alan.

Much of the time I spent in the classroom focused on locating the dominant heterosexual discourses, including how children embodied hegemonic masculinity and emphasized femininity. My observations tended to concentrate primarily on the children, the relationships they had with others in the classroom, and how these intersected with the heterosexual matrix. It was not until later in the study that I began recognizing how I was an active part of the heterosexual matrix. Reflecting in my daily research journal, I wrote:

> Something quite disturbing is happening while I'm "in the act" of researching in the classroom. Actually, it's my relationship with Alan that doesn't feel right. Why am I always so interested in his ideas, thoughts, and comments? What about the others in the classroom? It feels as though my whole research project is about Alan. Why is he the first student I look for when entering the classroom? Why do I tend to always notice and document his ideas first? Why do I find some students dull and boring, but never Alan? What might this mean? . . . What have I done? What am I a part of? If I consider Alan to be an example of hegemonic masculinity and if I'm always tempted to document his talk and actions rather than the others . . . Who gets left out, pushed to the margins . . . Oh my God, I'm part of it too! The heterosexual matrix is regulating who I am, what I document, and most likely my analysis! Hegemonic masculinity is seducing me! Is it controlling the study? This is disturbing . . . Can it [the heterosexual matrix] ever be disrupted?

This is the moment that I realized, *for myself*, the implications of the heterosexual matrix and how I was taking an active part in the social construction of gender. My awareness of the dominant nature of heterosexual discourses then helped me to refocus the ways in which I collected data. For example, before entering the classroom I reminded myself to concentrate on other children's talk and actions, not Alan's. I wrote myself a note, in large block letters, on the cover of my field notebook: "THIS STUDY IS NOT ABOUT ALAN!" In spite of these efforts, I found that after approximately 30 minutes of being in the classroom, most of the children had disappeared from my sight. That is, I caught myself wondering what Alan was doing in the classroom. I became conscious of how my body was physically turned toward Alan's play and I was actively listening for his voice. Although I was becoming aware of how my actions were connected to the heterosexual matrix, I was not prepared for the powerful ways in which it was also subverting the aims of the research project. I naively assumed that if I just worked harder at becoming neutral and objective, I would be able to remove myself from the heterosexual matrix.

Feeling Uncomfortable

Walkerdine's (1990) thought-provoking research conducted in a U.K. early childhood classroom highlights the gendered and sexualized nature of schooling. This work disturbingly shows how two young preschool boys, Terry and Sean, use their male power to silence and sexualize a female classmate and their female teacher, Miss Paxter. While researching, there were times when I found myself in similar situations with Alan. The following examples show how my research relationship with Alan was never objective, and at times uncomfortable.

> It is Story Partners, a time when the kindergarten class meets with second- and third-grade students for approximately 45 minutes to take part in shared reading. From across the room, I am watching Alan and Joey interact. Although I am far away and unable to hear all of their talk, I am able to see them and document their actions. Both boys are seated at the discovery table. They are not reading books. They both get up and head to the sink for a drink of water. At the sink, they begin playing around and then start spitting water into the sink. Joey keeps nervously looking around, especially toward the door, where the two head teachers are standing.
>
> Alan walks back to the discovery table and dramatically plops his body into the chair. He seems as though he is trying to get noticed. That is, he flings his arms back and kicks his feet up while jumping into the chair. Joey goes to look for a book. While waiting, Alan leans back in the chair, nonchalantly swinging his legs while looking around the room with an air of confidence. He soon starts kicking the wall with his feet. Joey returns and has selected four books to read. Alan looks at each

one, saying, "No . . . . . . no . . . . . . no . . . . . . a:n:d . . . no!" Joey
turns around and tries again to find some books that might
interest Alan.

While waiting for Joey, Alan continues looking around the
room. He notices me and from across the room catches my eye
and smiles. Then, using "big" motions, he leans back again in the
chair, crosses his arms, and says, "Mindy." He is motioning with
his hand for me to come over. I shake my head, pointing to my
notebook, and quickly say, "No, I'm busy researching." I then
look down at my notebook. Joey returns with two more books.
Alan shakes his head, saying, "No." Joey attempts a third time to
find a book that interests Alan. He returns, but with only one
book. Alan says, "No . . . Okay, you have *one more* chance."

Joey leaves to find another book but this time looks through a
different container. While Joey is searching for a book, Alan says
loudly from his seat, "Hey, Mindy. My story partner has disappeared." (He puts both of his hands out and looks around the
room) From across the room, Joey shows Alan the cover of a
book. Alan quickly glances toward Joey, saying, "Yuck!" while
trying to get my attention.

Throughout Story Partners, Alan skillfully directs his older story
partner's actions, never fully engaging in shared reading. By keeping his
story partner busy, Alan creates opportunities to establish a relationship
with me. Alan's cool and carefree attitude, emphasized as he leans back
in his chair and gazes across the room, is an example of how he is
choosing to perform a particular form of masculinity directed to and for
me. Alan wants to be the center of my attention, and he accesses positions of power in order to engage in heterosexual discourses. Although
I resist Alan's invitation to carry on a conversation through the crowded
classroom, by shaking my head, telling him no, and looking away, I still
found myself intrigued by Alan's actions. Both Alan and I are knowledgeable about these heterosexual discourses, and in taking part in
them, we are also constructing gender.

I remember feeling uncomfortable, as if something was not quite
right. I realized again what was happening and wrote in my field notes,
"I let it happen again. What is this all about? . . . I suck." As I revisit
this data, I find myself shaking my head slowly and saying, "I
can't believe this. Heteroreality is so hard to see past and even harder to

challenge." It is difficult to reread the transcripts because these moments remind me that I am not (and never will be) an objective researcher. It is clear that I have gender biases and preferences, forcing me to question the confines of heterosexual discourses in research. The social and political construction of gender is no longer an abstract concept happening to others. Instead, I am a part of a *heterosexualized* research relationship, and heteronormativity is playing out in my research. This moment also raises questions about my role as a female researcher conducting research with boys and girls. My sexual identity and gender performances influence research in several ways. For instance, it affects how I observe in the classroom, what talk and actions get noticed, and what gets written down.

Engaging in Heteronormative Discourses

Another example of the gendered and heterosexualized research relationship with Alan occurred while Alan and I were sitting out in the hall analyzing data. In this classroom, one student has the job of being the "teacher of the day." Responsibilities for this job include choosing stories and poems to be read during large group time, doing the calendar, and choosing partners when the entire class is required to line up and leave the room. My field notes indicate that when he is teacher of the day, Alan never pairs boys with girls. In order to understand Alan's partner pairing decisions, I shared my field notes with him regarding his partner choices.

Mindy: Do you remember when you were the teacher of the day and Isabel asked you to sit in the chair and said, "I want you to pick partners"? Do you remember that? I also wrote down who you chose and then I went home and typed it up on my computer.

Alan: Did you make a copy for me?

Mindy: Yes, I made a copy for you. (I hand him a copy of the list of partners) Plus I will make a copy of the tape today.

Alan: OK, so **I'm** the researcher (pointing to himself) and **I** (pointing to himself again) tell **you** (points to me) everything **I** (pointing to himself) know.

Mindy: Yes. So these are the pairs that you chose. (We go over the list together and he agrees that the partners are correct)

.

.

.

Mindy: When you decided to have Majindra go with Keith, was it something that you thought he wanted to do, or did you think that he wouldn't want to be with Keith?

Alan: It was **my** idea (pointing to himself). I didn't want it—it was something I want to do because **I** want to make this class, this whole class better.

Mindy: (Tone of voice changes and the pitch gets higher) *That's such a good idea, Alan! Wow. You are such a good thinker.*

Alan: Because if it's wrong, you know what's going to happen? (He stands up) People are going to be so:oo:oo strong! (Begins kicking the wall with his foot and making grunting noises)

Mindy: Okay, sit down, Alan. (Tone of voice changes, becoming softer) *So:ooo:ooo, if you're strong, though, are you bad?*

Alan: No, I'm not strong so well. I'm just strong.

Mindy: Who is the strongest in the class?

Alan: Oh, I'll tell you. (Sits down next to me on the floor) Raoul, Keith, James.

Mindy: Those are the three strongest boys?

Alan: Yeah.

Mindy: Who are the three strongest girls?

Alan: Nobody. (He is looking directly at me and his voice and facial expression indicate that I have asked a ridiculous question)

Mindy: None of the girls are strong?

Alan:	(Turns away from me, shrugging)
Mindy:	I saw some of those girls climbing that rope—they looked pretty strong.
Alan:	It was boys. Loren is strong.
Mindy:	Yeah, Loren is strong. But I also saw Breanna, Katy, and Penny climb the rope//
Alan:	//because they're {inaudible}.
Mindy:	That doesn't mean that they're strong?
Alan:	Nuh-uh. (Shakes head) If they're strong, they will have big, big, big muscles. (He bends his arm to show off his muscle, tenses his entire body)
Mindy:	And they shouldn't have big muscles?
Alan:	No, they **don't**. I don't see any. (Stands up, turns away, and begins kicking the wall)
Mindy:	(Tone of voice changes) *Have a seat, **please**. Now this is the other question I have. When I look at the pairs that you made, you have girls with girls and boys with boys. Did you do that on purpose?*
Alan:	Um, let me see. (Takes the list of names out of my hand and we go over the partner pairs together)
Mindy:	No boys and girls together.
Alan:	Because some I wanted to separate.
Mindy:	Oh, who did you want to separate?
Alan:	Here, let me show you. (Grabs the list out of my hands) Mary and Liza, because Mary was burning.
Mindy:	Burning? What does that mean?
Alan:	She was burning up. She was burning up mad.
Mindy:	Why was she mad?
Alan:	Maybe, no maybe. What is that? (Alan points to my handwriting, and the conversation turns to my note taking. I get the feeling that Alan is tired of this conversation, so it is ended.)

Although part of this discussion with Alan was used previously to show how Alan resists the idea that girls are physically capable in his classroom (see page 104), the full discussion also highlights our gendered power relationship. We both took part in heterosexual performances while sitting in the hall discussing data. These performances created and reinforced power relationships, which shifted throughout our conversation. Alan and I both gained and gave up power through our knowledge and use of heterosexual discourses. For example, Alan immediately gained power when he asked if I made a copy of my field notes for him. Although I attempted to create collaborative research relationships with a range of children in the classroom, not all would have taken me up on it in the way Alan did. With authority and confidence, Alan stated that he was going to tell me everything he knew. I then accepted his knowledge, supporting and valuing Alan's ability to work independently. As the discussion about his partner pairing decisions continued, it was important for Alan that I understand that these were *his* ideas. Soon, the power relationship between us changed. Again, I responded by recognizing and valuing his ideas. Each time that I responded, I supported rather than challenged our gendered power relationship. As illustrated throughout the transcription, the shaded areas show when I used my tone of voice to embody emphasized femininity. Instead of using a no-nonsense teacher voice to keep Alan in the game, I chose to use a more feminine tone of voice to keep him interested.

These examples show that Alan and I did not exist in a simple collaborative research relationship. Clearly, heteronormative practices existed while carrying out this project and are seen through the engagement that Alan and I had with heterosexual discourses. Being tempted by hegemonic masculinity and using emphasized femininity to engage Alan was not something that I anticipated would happen. Although it was initially hard to imagine how the heterosexual matrix could be regulating my research relationships with children, these uncomfortable moments that I experienced with Alan raise new questions about heterosexual discourses and its role in data collection.

The most noticeable way that heterosexual discourses influenced data collection was that I collected a lot more of it on Alan than on anyone else in the classroom. More field notes were taken about Alan, more audiotapes and videotapes were made of his talk and actions, and more of his drawings and writings were collected than was the case with any of the other children. What was most disturbing was not that I collected more data about Alan, but that I collected virtually nothing about the girls of color. I can't help but wonder about the messages I sent to both the girls and the boys in this classroom. By consistently focusing on Alan, I showed the class how I valued middle-class, Anglo-American boys and their ideas. My actions also told the class that I didn't think that the girls were as exciting or interesting. If heteronormativity, and my inability to disrupt it, prevents me from finding anything other than hegemonic masculinity worth investigating, then that is a serious limitation of my work.

Acts of Subversion

Through acts of subversion, Alan's beliefs about gender were questioned in the classroom. This section shows how a small group of girls and Isabel subverted Alan's dualistic thinking about gender as they worked collectively to create counterdiscourses in the classroom. While this section shows how the girls confront Alan with their actions and questions, it continues to disclose how my research relationship with Alan was gendered.

Counterdiscourses

As mentioned previously, discourses are ways of constituting or creating knowledge, including defining what it means to be gendered. Particular discourses offer a range of subject positions for girls and boys. While the dominant discourse offers a compulsory form of gender, its very organization also implies that other subject positions exist, including oppositional ways of being gendered. Counterdiscourses allow the disempowered subject of a discourse to speak in her own right, enabling girls to challenge gender norms and power. These alternative discourses also provide the discursive space from which individuals can resist dominant subject positions (Weedon, 1997). Isabel uses daily classroom practices, such as show-and-tell, to provide opportunities for dominant discourses to be challenged by the children. The following example of show-and-tell illustrates how gender norms can be exposed and then subverted by the children, showing all those involved that gender is not always so black and white, but rather is full of multiple, murky, and contradictory ways of being.

According to Weedon (1997), resisting the dominant discourse by individuals is the first step toward producing alternative forms of knowledge. Since children do have agency, they are able to resist dominant discourses and access counter ones. Isabel sees show-and-tell as a classroom routine that has the potential to create new ways of being gendered.

Early in the school year, Isabel was curious about the kinds of lunch boxes the children brought to school and suggested that I share my lunch bag for show-and-tell. Isabel thought that this kind of show-and-tell might elicit responses from the children about the genderedness of the lunch boxes that they brought to school.

> I place my brown lunch bag on the special block and explain that I reuse my lunch bag. James asks why I don't want to have a lunch box, and I reply that I just don't think about it, adding that a lunch box would be hard to fit in my backpack. Isabel then contributes, "I wonder about the lunch boxes I see every day. Students in this class all bring different kinds of lunch boxes." She holds up a red lunch box, asking, "Whose lunch box is this?" With the class sitting in a circle, Isabel holds all the other lunch boxes high up in the air in turn, and children claim their lunch box while telling us who chose it (i.e., themselves, Mom, or Dad) and why the lunch box was chosen.

Table 1 presents the information gathered during this show-and-tell session.

After all of the lunch boxes were placed in the middle of the rug, Isabel asked the class for their observations.

Isabel: Any noticings and observations? Nancy?

Nancy: Valerie and Katy's are the same, and Amy and Laura have the same.

Isabel: Sue.

Sue: There are seventeen lunch boxes.

Isabel: Katy.

Table 1 Lunch Box

Student	Lunch Box Description	Who Picked It Out?
Amy	*Arthur,* red color	Amy
James	Toy Story	James
Debbie	Pink with a plastic pocket for a photograph	Debbie ("But my mom decided to put my picture in it")
Liam	Blue background with yellow and red accent colors	Liam's mother
Kelly	Light purple (picture has rubbed off)	Kelly
Nancy	*Pocahontas* (with mirror and pocket for accessories)	Nicole ("It's like my book bag")
Laura	*Arthur,* red color	Laura
Ian	Blue nylon sack	Ian
Theresa	Bright pink	Theresa's mother ("Because the pink is like Barbie")
Holly	Princess from *Hercules*	Holly
Sue	Brightly colored cats	Sue's mother ("Because it's the same as my comforter at home")
Cheng	Primary colors, made of cloth	Cheng's mother
Madison	Winnie the Pooh	Madison ("Because I like Winnie the Pooh and I have the backpack")
Katy	Barbie	Katy ("I like Barbie")
Valerie	Barbie	Valerie's mother ("Because she knows that I like Barbie")
Alan	Toy Story	Alan ("Because I like the cartoon")
Kim	Light pink drink holder	Kim ("Because it was pink")

Katy: James and Alan have the same kind of lunch boxes, Buzz Lightyear and {inaudible}.

Valerie: (Whispering to Kim, while pointing to the lunch boxes) Whoa, look at the boys' lunch boxes!

Isabel: I think that these (standing in the middle of the rug pointing to a group of lunch boxes) are about colors. Debbie.

Debbie: Mine is kind of like Barbie.

Isabel: Katy.

Katy: Yeah, it's kind of like the Ballerina Barbie.

Isabel: Cheng.

Cheng: (He comments on the different shapes of the lunch boxes. His English is limited and he must point to the lunch boxes in order to be understood.)

Isabel: Madison.

Madison: (Gets up and walks to her lunch box) Mine is kind of blue if I turned it this way. (She turns lunch box, then stands up, looking at Isabel, and smiles) Hey! We could make a Disney section! (She groups some of the lunch boxes)

Isabel: What about this? (Reorganizes lunch boxes) I could put all of the lunch boxes that are just colored here. Oh, look, this is a girl (*Pocahontas* lunch box), girl (Barbie lunch box). What do I do about this one? (Holds up the *Arthur* lunch box for everyone to see)

Alan: How about one goes into the girl and one into the boys?

Isabel: What do you mean?

Alan: Well, make a boy pile and a girl one.

Isabel: What about Winnie the Pooh?

Class: Boy.

Isabel: He is a boy? How do you know?

Debbie: Because he has a movie.

Isabel: Because he has a movie? I don't understand.

Keith: Pooh has a boy voice.

Katy: *Well, I heard a tape and it sounded like a boy, but it was a girl!* (moving head back and forth, with a "know-it-all" voice)

Sue: What Katy said is true.

Keith: Pooh is a boy because of his hair. He has hair like a boy.

Katy: It doesn't depend on the hair. **I've** seen boys with long hair.

Madison: Yeah.

Cheng: It's his voice, voice.

Alan: Pooh's name is a boy name.

Madison: (Rises to her knees and then slowly stands up, voice get-
           ting louder, a determined look on her face) How about if
           your name was Kelly? (Looking at and pointing to Kelly,
           who is sitting on the circle) That could be a boy or a girl.
           So Winnie could be either a boy or a girl name.

The conversation continues about Arthur's dog, Pal. The class
decides that the gender of the dog (which they mistakenly assign as
female; in the show Pal is a male) would determine where the lunch box
would be placed. Isabel then changes the direction of the discussion by
re-sorting the lunch boxes into boxes that girls would carry and boxes
that boys would carry. She asks the class if a boy would carry the pink
Barbie lunch box.

Alan: (Shaking his head and moving hands back and forth) **No
           way!** Boys are not **allowed** to play with Barbies.

Debbie: Well, my brother plays with Barbies.

Alan: He's a baby.

Katy: **Hey,** my brother is eight years old and he plays with Bar-
           bies.

Alan: (Shrugs while shaking his head)

Show-and-tell provides the opportunity for a range of perspectives
about gender to emerge in a public space, including gender stereotypes
and contradictions about gender norms. For example, there is the belief
that there are definite and distinct boy and girl lunch boxes, that some
lunch boxes would not be carried by boys, and that Winnie the Pooh is
a boy. At the same time, these gender norms are challenged when Katy,
Sue, and Madison rely on their own experiences with gender to explain
that having a particular voice, haircut, or name does not determine if
you are a girl or a boy. Also, Katy challenges Alan's belief that boys are
not allowed to play with Barbies as she uses her older brother as an
example of a boy who does play with dolls. Although Katy, Madison,

and Sue are working collectively to subvert the dominant discourse, it is not certain that they have made a difference in Alan's understandings about gender.

It is interesting how Alan suggests that the lunch boxes be grouped according to gender. In doing so, he attempts to reinforce gender differences. It is not until the class is confronted with two identical Arthur lunch boxes that they begin to consider the possibility of a lunch box belonging to both groups. Since the two Arthur lunch boxes belong to Amy and Laura, it seems logical to place them in the girl lunch box pile. Based on the concept of fairness, Alan suggests that one Arthur lunch box be placed in the boy pile and one placed in the girl pile. However, there is further discussion about the placement of these lunch boxes, and it is determined that they will be placed in each category because there is one female character and one boy character. That is, since Arthur is a boy and (the children think) his dog Pal is a girl, it is only fair that one lunch box be placed in the girls pile and the other in the boys'.

The discussion becomes more intriguing as children actively struggle with the gender contradictions presented before them on the rug. For instance, the class initially agrees that the character Winnie the Pooh is a boy because of his voice and short hair. However, Katy disagrees, drawing from her life experiences to explain that sometimes a voice might sound like a boy's voice, but in fact it can be a girl's. Katy continues with this line of reasoning by showing more gender contradictions found in her everyday world. Regardless of Katy's anecdotes, Alan firmly believes that Winnie the Pooh is a boy. For Alan, there are particular and right ways to be a boy.

Madison, whom you will meet in Chapter 6, is another classmate who challenges Alan's rigid beliefs about gender differences. First, she uses the example of Kelly, a female classmate who is sitting next to Alan in the circle, to show that Kelly's name is gender-neutral. Second, she physically positions herself above Alan, towering over him, while raising her voice in order to strongly make her point. It seems as though both Katy and Madison are able to live with gender ambiguities, or at least allow themselves to see that gender norms are not so "normal." Finally, as Alan is challenged with these gender contradictions taken from his classmates' lived experiences, he does not know what to do.

His understandings about gender may be contested as he is confronted once again by Katy as she explains that her older brother plays with Barbie dolls. Alan's knowledge of gender norms and his insistence on maintaining them creates conflict when he is opposed by Katy's counterdiscourse, and ultimately he is positioned as powerless. However, another reading of Alan's response is that he is anything but powerless. Instead, he cleverly uses silence as a form of power. Most of the class will concur in his silencing of these alternative ways of seeing gender. As a result of Alan's silence, gender discourses are not subverted, but rather maintained, with hegemonic masculinity and emphasized femininity remaining intact.

Overt Interventions

Although Isabel believes that certain classroom structures and routines support counterdiscourses, there are also instances where she finds it necessary to overtly intervene in order to actively oppose hegemonic masculinity. The following example occurred during work share. At this time of the school year, it was Loren's responsibility to guide and direct the children.

> It is work share, and children are seated on the rug. Loren asks the group she was cooking with earlier to stand in front of the class and share how they helped make haroseth during center time. The group stands in front of the class in the following order: Alan, Nancy, Majindra, and Ian. Nancy is not standing with the group. Instead, she has moved in back of Alan and Majindra, and they have quickly taken over her spot.

Loren: Going down from Alan, to Nancy, Majindra, and then Ian, say two things that you did while making haroseth.

Isabel: Ian, let's hear one thing.

Ian: We started cutting apples and then it got sticky and we cut dates.

Isabel: Majindra.

Majindra: We cut apples on a plate and then we got dates.

Isabel: Nancy—stand up, Nancy. Stand up straight like Ian.

Alan:	I'll tell you everything. (Pushes Nancy to the side and moves his body in front of Nancy)
Isabel:	No, Nancy is speaking.
Alan:	But maybe she forgot.
Isabel:	Come on, Nancy. Stand up.
Loren:	Say one thing that you can do. Remember how we mixed the haroseth?
Alan:	And we also put grape juice and we put the whole thing together.
Loren:	So you eat haroseth and then the matzo?
Alan:	No, you put the haroseth **on** the matzo and then you **eat** the matzo in little pieces.
Isabel:	So you break off a piece of matzo and put a little bit of haroseth on it and eat it, then break off another piece of matzo and put more haroseth on it?
Alan:	You can't have another piece of um, um, um, matzo.

As this group of children stands in front of the class waiting to share, they have situated themselves in a line. Usually if a group is sharing, they tend to start from the left of the line and proceed to the right. Knowing this informal rule, Alan has strategically positioned himself to share first. However, Isabel's overt interventions prevent this, and she tells Ian to begin. Ensuring that Alan does not take over work share, Isabel uses her authority as the teacher and calls on each child to share. Conscious of Nancy's attempts to disappear, Isabel clearly tells Nancy to stand up when presenting to the class. At this point, Alan uses his body to push Nancy aside so that he can be seen and have his ideas heard. Again Isabel quickly intervenes, preventing Alan's voice from being the only one heard. These interventionist strategies are used by Isabel to subvert hegemonic masculinity and allow other ideas to be heard. Even so, Alan successfully resists Isabel's strategies and ultimately marginalizes Nancy. For example, not only does Alan push Nancy back, but he also states that he will tell the class everything, implying that he is the expert. Instead of accepting Isabel's statement "No, Nancy is speaking," Alan skillfully suggests that she might have left out some vital information, implying that girls could never know as much as he does.

Another overt intervention occurred when Isabel made "hidden work" explicit for the entire class. Isabel is aware of how Alan values explicit and individual work, and when she noticed him doing invisible work with others in the classroom, she was quick to highlight and appreciate these endeavors.

> Children are sitting on the rug and Isabel is in her blue chair. Isabel begins work share by talking about invisible work. In a serious voice, she places both hands on her knees and leans slightly forward, saying, "You know how I've talked about doing invisible work? Well, today I saw students doing important invisible work. Today during cleanup, Ian and Alan both committed themselves to cleaning up the sand table areas together. While Alan swept, Ian held the dust pan. Hot stuff!" She smiles, looking at them both, while giving them thumbs-up signs with both hands.

Isabel purposely uses a combination of strategies to challenge Alan's rigid understandings of gender. For Isabel, work share and show-and-tell are two classroom routines that provide opportunities for intentionally inserting counterdiscourses into the curriculum for Alan, and others, to explore. As these classroom scenes show, Isabel is not passive about confronting gender issues in the classroom. Instead, she attempts to use her authority and power as the teacher in order to challenge the investment that children such as Alan have in hegemonic masculinity and the heterosexual matrix. Furthermore, by having children talk about their experiences, they are learning how to question and challenge the status quo. Even though not all of her interventions are successful, Isabel works hard at confronting and challenging gender inequity in her classroom. A teacher operating from a developmental perspective will not see gender in the same way that Isabel does. Instead, Isabel's interests in gender and equity enable her to highlight children's talk and actions that most teachers overlook or see as insignificant.

This chapter shows the various ways in which Alan experiences being a boy in this classroom. Even though Alan attempts to enact hegemonic masculinity, he is not always positioned as powerful in this classroom. For example, when he is confronted by counterdiscourses, he experiences briefly what it feels like to be pushed to the margins. When challenged by certain girls, Alan begins to realize what it is like when others successfully contest his power. The defenses that Alan utilizes when feeling powerless include his body language, physical assertiveness, and silence. Mostly though, this case study discloses Alan working hard to position others as powerless. Alan is considered a power broker because of the efforts he makes to use power to support and maintain gender differences. He skillfully uses his knowledge and understandings of gender to position others through the heterosexual matrix, constructing males and females in limited ways.

Implications for Early Childhood Teaching and Research

The discoveries that I made with Alan have implications for teaching and researching in early childhood education. Most teaching and researching practices do not set out to document the gendered and often problematic relationships that adults have with children. Deliberately setting out to document these uncomfortable moments that we frequently encounter in practice is one step toward uncovering the complicated ways that gender heterosexualizes relationships. However, as my experiences reveal, this is not an easy task. Not only will it take vigilance, but it is essential that it be built into our teaching plans and research designs if we are committed to promoting equity and social justice in early childhood classrooms.

Documenting these gendered relationships provokes new directions for collaborative research and teaching. This means bringing up uncomfortable gender moments with children and raising new questions with them about these power relationships. Until we gain confidence with this new role, these interventions might first occur after a critical event happens around gender issues. It often took time for me to realize how heterosexism was playing out in my relationships with children. I then needed additional time to strategize how I was going to attend to these uncomfortable moments in my practice as a researcher. After recognizing that I was collecting more information on the boys, and in particular Alan, I could then show the class how much data I had collected in the classroom. Next, I might display the stacks of data I had gathered and compare the amounts I collected on the boys with the girls. The class would immediately see that I was not collecting equal amounts of information about all of the children. I would then ask the class for their opinions regarding this phenomenon and seek suggestions of how to proceed.

When Alan and I were in the hallway analyzing video data, I could have immediately acknowledged, exposed, and contested his violent actions (MacNaughton, 2000). Instead, I relied on what I know best, emphasized femininity, to stop his hegemonic masculine behaviors. This of course did not work and only maintained gender norms and the heterosexual matrix. I could have attempted to shut him down by saying. 'No! Stop that!" However this would merely have been an attempt to maintain my power as an adult, rather than raising the issue of gender. A better response would be to state, "Alan, I need you to stop kicking the wall, it is making me feel uncomfortable. I think that you are doing that because I am a girl and that sometimes makes you angry. I also think that you are kicking the wall because you think that it is okay for boys to act in those ways. I want you to find a different way to be a boy. I know that when Ian is upset he takes a deep breath, counts to ten, and then shares how he is feeling. I know that Ian is being courageous when he acts in that way."

Exposing the gender politics of these relationships will not be easy for teachers, researchers, or children. As MacNaughton's (2000) work with early childhood teachers working toward gender equity has shown, those that attempt to challenge hegemonic masculinity often find it problematic. Not only does this kind of work take us away from focusing on the girls, but the boys usually resist. Therefore, it is necessary for teachers to remember that challenging hegemonic masculinity will always be daunting, but this work is vital if we are interested in dismantling heteronormativity in the early childhood classroom.

5

MADISON: A RISK TAKER

In chapter 4 we met Alan, who in many ways can be considered a "typical" boy who has realized the privilege, prestige, and power of hegemonic masculinity. This chapter introduces Madison, an "atypical" girl who defies gender norms. This chapter shows how Madison is also a gender expert, using her knowledge about gender discourses to be the kind of girl that she wants to be. In doing so, Madison takes risks by exploring a range of ways of being a girl. These alternative ways that Madison does gender occur through the counterdiscourses that she creates and enters through her play in the classroom. Integrated throughout this chapter are examples of how Isabel and some children support Madison's attempts at resisting gender norms.

Subverting Gender Expectations

Madison enters the classroom with energy and self-confidence. She is an active participant in the classroom community, getting along well with both the adults and the children in her classroom. Madison has lots of friends and seems to play with everyone. Madison's uniqueness lies in her ability not only to understand the ambiguities of gender, but also to successfully challenge them in her daily life. While Madison experiments with what it means to be a girl, she is also catching on to the politics of gender within the classroom and larger society. While learning about the complexities of gender norms, she works hard at questioning and subverting them through her talk and play. Madison knowingly and willingly takes risks while challenging what it means to be a girl in this classroom.

Madison is Anglo-American and part of a working-class family consisting of herself and a mother and father who both work full time. Although Madison is the only child living at home, she talks about Kevin, an older brother who lives in another state. Madison's mother is conscious of women's issues, a fact that surfaced before the school year officially began. As a way of introducing the new kindergarten children to their teachers, families are asked by the school's principal to write a letter describing what makes their child special and the story behind their name. In the hallway, I noticed a framed photograph of Madison and the letter written by her mother disclosing that Madison was named after a famous female political figure's daughter. Madison's mother wrote how she respects this female politician and believes her to be a strong and powerful woman. She thought that if this particular feminist could name her child Madison, then so could she.

Madison spends the bulk of her time with other children, attending before- and after-school child care. She is around a range of people and social situations each day, and I observed her getting along well with others. In the classroom, Madison is seen solving social problems independently, rarely seeking out adults to help settle her disagreements. Instead of "telling" on a classmate, Madison simply works out problems on her own, rather than relying on discourses that frequently position girls as helpless. For example, during cleanup time in dramatic play, Theresa walked slowly around in circles, avoiding the task of picking up. Instead of telling one of the adults in the classroom about this, Madison walked up to Theresa and said firmly, "You are not cleaning up and it's not fair! If you're going to play here with us, you need to help. Okay?"

Occasionally, Madison can be regarded as a 6-year-old activist. While Alan spends his time in kindergarten maintaining gender norms, Madison works hard at dismantling normative ways of being a girl for herself and others. In the classroom, I observed Madison high-lighting for her peers the gender inequities that exist in the classroom and society. For example, as the poem, "Peter, Peter, Pumpkin Eater" was read out loud during morning meeting, she had a puzzled look on her face when she heard that Peter kept his wife in a pumpkin shell. Madison wondered out loud, "Huh? What?" After reading the poem, Isabel asked Madison if there was anything wrong, and she replied, "Well, I don't think that's fair. I mean, would you want to stay inside of a pumpkin cleaning and cooking all day?"

Multiple Identities

Madison's identity as a girl seems neither fixed nor stable, and at times it seems to have contradictory elements. For example, at one moment Madison is seen playing at Lego, and later that afternoon she is at the writing center with a group of girls, making heart-filled drawings, done decoratively in a variety of shades of pink. Exploring what influences Madison's decisions helps us to understand the complexities of gender discourses. That is, why does Madison decide to immerse herself in two dramatically different forms of play? Does every child do this? Why are these actions considered "normal" by some children but are a big deal for others?

What it means to be a girl for Madison is constantly changing and is difficult to define through the concepts of either a "girly girl" or a "cool girl." Although these examples of femininity are helpful for locating gender, they are limiting when trying to understand Madison's multi-ple gender identities. For example, I do not consider Madison to be either a girly girl or a cool girl. At the same time, I also do not think of her as a tomboy. Her long, light brown hair is rarely brushed, and her wrinkled clothes make her look a bit disheveled. She is not unclean, but she looks unkempt, as if she has just rolled out of bed. Madison is phys-ically active, is often seen taking part in rough-and-tumble play, and therefore dresses so that she can easily move about and get messy. The holes in her stretch pants are a result of her style of play. Staying clean, neat, and looking pretty is *usually* not a concern of Madison, and she *usually* does not wear skirts or dresses to school. I stress the word *usually* because wearing dresses, playing with dolls, or spending time talking about boyfriends are not regular actions for Madison. Therefore, I was shocked on the one and only day when I saw Madison wearing a dress—not because she was in a dress, but because she was wearing an overtly feminized and "girly" red velvet dress with pink tights. At first, Madison's outfit caught me off guard, but then I realized that this was just another example of Madison "doing" gender. Toward the end of the day, I asked Madison about her dress, and she explained, "Oh, this thing (pointing to her dress)? I just wanted to wear it. Sometimes I choose, no I mean, I like to wear dresses." This moment forced me to think about the expectations I had of Madison and the way I valued particular gender performances. Why was I so surprised to see her in this particular dress? Did I believe that Madison only performed particular forms of femininity? If I really wanted to know more about Madison's gender, I should have asked her why she wore the dress, how wearing it made her feel, and if wearing it prevented and/or allowed her access to different discourses. Maybe Madison chose to wear the dress because on that day it gave her access to particular discourses and power in the classroom. But we should also remember that Madison deserves the space to wear what she likes; on some occasions a dress might just be a dress, rather than a significant symbol of femininity.

Madison seems to rely on a set of inner resources that give her the strength needed to take gender risks. One day Madison approached the dramatic play center, attempting to enter into Alan and Ian's play. Unlike other children who might stand on the sidelines, waiting to be invited into the play, Madison confidently walked straight into the dramatic play center and asked if she could be the dog. Alan said, "No. We don't need a dog . . . In fact, we don't **want** a dog." Madison then offered to be the baby. Again, Alan rejected her idea. Some children would have immediately gone and told Isabel that the boys were not letting them play. However, Madison chose to walk away, going to the art table instead. When asked why she did not stay long in dramatic play, she simply stated, "Because of Alan." I wonder what Madison learned from this interaction. From watching her over time, I believe that she realizes that even if an adult intervenes, it will not be satisfying play. However, there is more to it than this. Alan does not include Madison because she challenges his fixed notions of gender, seeing her as a threat to his power. Someone like Valerie might well have been less threatening and therefore might have been included.

Getting Sweaty

Madison does not write stories, poems, or books about feminine subjects such as dolls, makeup, or princesses. Instead, she spends writing workshop writing about basketball, pets, after-school care, or the rides at Disneyland. The following book, written and published during writing workshop and part of the classroom library, is one example of Madison's writing.

Basketball

Basketball.

The basketball is in the hoop. Yes, yes, yes.

Coach says breakout time.

I am playing basketball and Daddy too.

I love basketball.

I scored a point. Yes, yes, yes.

Interested in the genderedness of the books that children were writing, I collected several, including Madison's book *Basketball*, and asked the children to read their books out loud. The following transcript is of Madison reading her book out loud and describing the illustrations.

Mindy: Madison, could you read your book to me?

Madison: Sure. (Takes her book, opens it, and begins reading) Basketball. Basketball is in the hoop. Yes, yes, yes. (Stops and points to some of the pictures and begins explaining them) This is me, this is my brother, and this is my hair . . . it's staticky. (Turns the page) Coach says breakout time.

Mindy: What does that mean?

Madison: When you're so sweaty, when you go and shower and get drinks, that's what a breakout is. (Looks back at the book and continues reading) Basketball. (Stops and points to the drawings) The world's longest basketball. Me cheating and my daddy grabs me.

Mindy: How are you cheating?

Madison: I jump to catch the basketball, my hands are in the hoop, and my whole body is in the hoop (laughing) and I try and catch the basketball. (Pointing to her drawing) Me. (Starts reading again) I am playing basketball and Daddy too. I love basketball. (Pointing to the drawing) Me. A basketball on top of my head. (Finishes reading) I scored a point. Yes, yes, yes.

Not only does Madison write about the sport of basketball, but she also draws herself playing the game. As a basketball player, Madison does not appear to have the feminine qualities associated with the girly girls or the cool girls. Instead, she jumps, catches, shoots baskets, and gets sweaty. This book about basketball is another example of how Madison enacts femininity. For Madison, being a girl is not based on looking beautiful. Instead, this form of femininity is about getting involved in sports and playing with the boys. Although playing basketball might be a difficult discourse for some girls, it is not an issue for Madison. Instead, Madison likes playing basketball and the power that she feels while engaging in this activity. However, if boys are not attracted to this kind of femininity, then this form of femininity does not exist within the heterosexual matrix. By taking herself out of heteronormative discourses, Madison does gender differently than most of the girls in her class.

How Other Girls Viewed Madison

Although I was gaining a sense of Madison's ability to understand and do gender differently when compared with the other children in the class, I was also curious about what her classmates thought. Did they see her in similar ways? Would they value Madison's abilities as a risk taker, challenging and questioning gender? One morning I asked Sue about some of the books that the girls in her class were writing. I showed her Madison's book, *Basketball,* and Penny's book, *Dolls.* After she looked at both books, I asked Sue if she thought Madison would ever write a book about dolls. At first Sue was not sure. But then she explained, "Well, Madison likes to do all sorts of things. So she **might** write a book about dolls, but probably not . . . Just like she probably wouldn't write about fairies or princesses either." Sue understands that Madison is clever about gender and writes about topics and subjects that are not overtly feminine but which interest her.

Returning to the conversation I had with Liza and Katy about fashion girls allows us to see that Madison is not considered to be a fashion girl by two of her classmates.

Mindy: Would Madison be a fashion girl?

Liza: No, she always wears jeans and things like that.

Katy: W:e:l:l, Theresa is not **really** a fashion girl. She always wears like pants and shirts and not really dresses. Sometimes I wear dresses.

Mindy: In order to be a fashion girl do you have to wear dresses?

Katy: Yes. Wait, actually you can be a fashion girl and not wear a dress. Liza is a fashion girl and she isn't wearing a dress. But um, Theresa wears things that don't add up. Like, she wears a green shirt and purple pants. These (pointing to her clothes) add up because this (pointing to her pants) is blue and this (pointing to her top) is purple.

We can see here that Madison's classmates understand clearly the sorts of clothes that she wears. Jeans are practical clothing, allowing Madison to engage in all sorts of active and messy play. As the conversation continues we see that Katy has a nuanced understanding of gendered clothing. Stereotypically, we would expect fashion girls to wear dresses and skirts. However, even kindergarteners know that it is not that simple. As Katy's comments show, she and others understand that powerful forms of femininity can be performed by wearing shirts and pants—that is, as long as they match!

Engineering Her Desires

At the beginning of the school year, I observed that Madison was the only girl who regularly visited the table toy center during center time.

When asked, Madison happily explains that her favorite learning center is table toys, where she plays with Lego. When watching Madison choose where she will play during center time, it is apparent that she bases her center time choices on her interests and desires. When Madison chooses to play with Lego, it is because this is what she wants to do, not because a friend is playing there.

For Madison, the easiest thing for her at school is "playing with Lego because you just push!" Not only is Lego easy for Madison, but she is also skilled at it. I often observed her creating complex three-dimensional buildings and objects out of Lego. One day, during center time, I played and talked with Madison, Raoul, James, and Keith at the table toy center. Madison was seated next to Keith, and they were engaged in fantasy play, involving bad guys, fire, and dungeons. Madison was building a house with Lego. Her structure was divided by walls, containing six separate rooms, including a dungeon for bad guys. There were four male Lego action figures within her structure.

Mindy: What does a bad guy have to do to be bad?

Madison: He's got to kill to you.

Raoul: And he plays with you if you say you're not going to the bad guys' hideout.

Madison: Yeah, 'cause you're gonna have to kill me first. So, and then before you move, you go (demonstrates how to make Lego figures fight). (To me) When the bad guy comes over, you dial 911, okay?

.

.

.

Madison: Yeah, fire him, he's killing him 'cause he's a bad guy (making Lego boy and snake fight).

Keith: (Makes shooting noises, begins talking in a creepy monster voice) ***Yeah. I can blow fire.***

Madison: I can **become** fire//

Keith: (Creepy monster voice) ***I got you on fire.***

Madison: No, but I can blow fire too. **And** at the same time as snakes.

Keith: Pretend we was friends, but, but I'm not a bad guy and you're not a bad guy, okay?

Madison: Yeah but pretend we **are** bad guys, and I'm just a little bit of a bad guy and { }.

As their play continues it intensifies in both action and sound. Bad guys are tricked and thrown into dungeons, and 911 is called several times for help. They become very excited and begin interrupting each other as their Lego action figures fight.

This episode illustrates Madison as a competent Lego builder and player. She is comfortably immersed within what is regarded as the masculine world of Lego. That is, she is playing at a "boy" center, interacting with masculinized toys, and engaging in violent and aggressive play with three other boys. Although female action figures are available, Madison chooses not to play with them. The play becomes intense and aggressive, as the "bad guys" fight, kill, shoot, blow fire, and transform. Madison chooses to play this way because it affirms her desires. She seeks out play that interests and excites her. She does not want to be limited by traditional female scripts. Madison wants to be herself, and the self she wants to be does not exist within the discourses of emphasized femininity or hegemonic masculinity. Playing with the boys generates a new discourse in the classroom, one in which boys and girls can play similar games with similar enjoyment. Although Madison appears to be enacting forms of hegemonic masculinity in her Lego play, they take on different meanings for her. Whereas Alan might use hegemonic masculinity to exclude others, Madison uses this discourse to strategically access power for herself. It is using power for herself, rather than using power over others.

Conversations with children confirmed my observations of Madison as one of the few girls who played at the table toy center with Lego. Although Madison's classmates usually considered her to be a good Lego builder, the following conversation shows otherwise.

Mindy: (Looking at Madison) Who do you think is the best Lego builder in the classroom?

Raoul: James.

Madison: James.

Mindy: Not Keith?

Raoul: No.

Mindy: Not Madison?

Madison: Me **and** James.

Raoul: Yeah.

James: And you (pointing to me)?

Mindy: Oh no, I'm not a good builder.

Madison: I'm not either. You know what? (Picks up a male action Lego figure and makes him move back and forth) He is a good fixer.

The dominant paradigm, that girls don't play with Lego, prevents Madison from immediately being recognized as a competent Lego builder. For example, although Raoul and James agree that Madison is a good Lego builder, she is not mentioned first. Unfortunately, my response about not being a good Lego builder reinforces the myth that girls don't or can't do Lego. In fact, after I make this statement, Madison changes her mind about her building capabilities, suggesting that it is really the male Lego action figure who is a good fixer. Although the class knows and sees Madison and me as capable and competent Lego players, both Madison and I slip into normative ways of being female. This is how discourses grow, and how we take an active part in constructing what it means to be female and male. By failing to challenge the idea that girls are good builders and Lego players, Madison and I maintain gender norms, letting others at the table believe that we are unable to take part in the boys' world of Lego.

Girls "Taking Over" Lego

Although I knew of Madison's involvement with Lego, I was unaware of how she actively encouraged more girls to join her at the table toy center until I observed her approach Sue, asking, "Hey, Sue, do you want to come and build at Lego? It's really fun." Sue replied, "I don't know. I'm not very good at it. Besides, all the boys go there." Madison then turned around and headed to table toys, saying over her shoulder, "Give it a try. I bet you'll love it."

Throughout the school year, Madison continues to encourage and support the girls to give the "boy center" a try. Her efforts paid off when she and three other girls "took over" Lego by using the classroom rule of making a reservation. In this class, children are allowed to save a spot at a particular center by writing a note and making a reservation. Knowing this rule, as well as knowing that most of the boys in her class aren't willing to or can't write a note, Madison prevents the boys from playing at this center.

Morning Meeting as a Political Site of Struggle

Over time, more girls begin frequenting the table toy center to play with Lego and actively making a group reservation of four girls, enabling them to control this learning center. As a result of the girls taking over Lego, a few boys had a difficult time handling their disappointment. Although Isabel originally decided to use morning meeting to talk about this phenomenon with the entire class, she turned it into a political site of struggle.

Isabel: I have a note that Valerie, Breanna, Sue, and Debbie are going to Lego. (Holds it up and shows it to the class)

Alan: **Oh no!** (Dramatically closes his eyes while placing both of his hands over them and slumping)

Isabel: That means that Lego will be closed because it will be taken up by the four people who already made a reservation. When you write me a note, that means you've made a reservation for that spot. And if I have Valerie, Breanna, Sue, and Debbie, I have a reservation for four at table toys. That means that table toys is closed up. And Mindy said, "Isabel, this is very interesting. What do you think will happen when those boys who expect to go to Lego, what do you think they'll do?" What do you think will happen tomorrow when it's almost center time and those boys will say, "Oh dear, what shall we do?" Sue, do you have an idea of what they might do?

Sue: Maybe, the, um, they want to go somewhere else, their second choice.

Isabel: What do you think that one might be?

Sue: It might be sand or dramatic play.

Isabel: It can't be blocks, because Kelly and Madison have made a reservation to continue the building//

Alan: //Isabel.

Isabel: //of the *Titanic* . . . Alan, did you have something to say? Raise your hand. Cheng.

Cheng: Why can't I go to Lego? I want to go to Lego every day.

Isabel: I know you do, but somebody else made a reservation. So what are you thinking about, Cheng, that you can do, since you won't be able to go to Lego? Think about that. Alan?

Alan: Um, Isabel, well, every girl always gets to go to blocks and boys never get to go.

Isabel: Would you like a reservation at blocks?

Alan: Yes, every time I raise my hand and try to go to blocks but every time it's Holly, Kim, or somebody else.

Isabel: Well, Alan, if you can get a partner, someone you'd like to go to blocks with and make a reservation, then when Madison and Kelly are finished with their project you'll be next with a reservation.

Isabel begins this meeting by briefly explaining the history of how a group of four girls, originally led by Madison, have come to monopolize Lego, preventing other children from playing there. Immediately, Alan responds with his body and tone of voice by showing the class his disappointment that the girls have taken over Lego. As the discussion continues, it becomes apparent that Isabel will allow these four girls to remain at Lego. Some teachers, working from an equal-opportunities approach, might agree with Alan, believing that allowing the girls to take over Lego is not fair. However, Isabel is working from an equity standpoint and sees this as fair play for the girls. That is, she recognizes the importance of allowing the girls to take over Lego and being able to play at a masculinized center on their own terms. It is apparent that Alan is upset with Isabel's decision, and he works hard trying to get Isabel to change the current discourse. Anything other than absolute power feels unfair for hegemonic masculinity. As the class meeting continues, Isabel uses this time to help some of the boys work through their disappointment about not being able to play with Lego.

Isabel: Cheng, what do you enjoy when you can't go to Lego?

Cheng: I like to go to dramatic play, but I really, really, really, really like Lego.

Isabel: Now, let's just say that before I call on you, three people say dramatic play. Let's make believe that it's tomorrow. Let's pretend it's tomorrow and three people already say dramatic play, and then I say, "Cheng?" Will you cry again?

Cheng: (Quietly) *No.*

Isabel: Remember the day you cried?

Cheng: (Quietly and looking away) *I know.*

Isabel: And now you know how to handle the disappointment better. Where do you think you might go? Where do you think Cheng would enjoy being?

Keith: Sand.

Isabel: So you think he might choose sand.

Keith: Yeah, I would be there with him if he cries.

Isabel: And you would help him handle his disappointment? Because last time he was really crying and you helped him handle his disappointment.

Keith: Yeah, I handled it.

After helping Cheng and other boys who are challenged by the girls occupying Lego, Isabel redirects the conversation to focus again on the girls and how they collectively began visiting Lego.

Isabel: Since September at Lego, September boys in Lego, October boys in Lego, November, December, January, February, six months it was mostly boys in Lego, in

March a couple of girls started to go to Lego. I wonder why that started to happen. How did it happen that all of a sudden one girl started//

Madison: //Isabel.

Isabel: You're right.//

Sue: //I know why. Me and Valerie were at dollhouse and since two of them had to leave from Lego, we asked you, me and Valerie asked you if we could go to Lego. So we started something and then Breanna //wanted and then she came.

Breanna: //I came to Lego because I wanted to make some// So I just got

Isabel: So it was a social decision. Wait, I made a mistake. Most of the time there were boys in Lego **except** Madison went to Lego quite a few times and every once in a while Breanna would go to work on this (shows Breanna's red/white structure). Now that I'm remembering, every once in a while Breanna would go to work on this and quite often Madison would work there and that was so important because it was because of **you** (looking at Madison) that we wrote the letter to the Lego people.

Breanna: And I had to go back there because I was at Lego and Valerie wanted to come and she asked me if she could and I said yes. And then Valerie, Sue, and me worked at Lego.

Isabel: Now, Valerie and Sue, you were at dollhouse. Was there anything that made you interested with Lego, so that when two people left that center you were interested in playing there? What made you interested?

Valerie: It was because dollhouse was getting real boring because it was getting real noisy and people would peek in through the windows. It was when people left that we decided to go to Lego.

Isabel: Now when you went there, did you enjoy what you were doing there and that made you want to go back again?

Valerie: Yes. And then when Sue and Breanna went to Lego it was awesome.

Isabel is using her knowledge of Madison's involvement in Lego to raise all the children's awareness of the current gender politics circulating in the classroom. Asking the girls to retell their Lego stories allows everyone to hear about, and perhaps appreciate, their attempts at playing with Lego. When asked why they started going to Lego, the girls frame their responses around social decisions, because their friends were at this center playing. However, these answers might indicate that the girls do not feel able to say, "I want to go to Lego." Choosing to go and play at Lego, with the boys, might be too risky for some of the girls in this classroom. Isabel then talks about how she noticed that Madison was one of the first girls to work at Lego and how her inquiries played an important part in writing a letter to the company that makes Lego.

The Gendered Curriculum

As morning meeting continued, Isabel focused on the genderedness of the learning centers in the classroom. She did this by asking about which learning centers the girls and boys like the most.

Isabel: Do you think that there are any other centers that are mostly for boys?

Breanna: Besides Lego?

Sue: Not including Lego?

Isabel: That's interesting . . . (Looking over to me with a puzzled look) Is Lego the top center for boys?

Breanna: I think most of the boys, not all the boys, but most like to go to Lego.//

Katy: //**Dramatic** play too. Dramatic play.

Isabel: Majindra, what's your best center?

Majindra: Um, reading on the rug. Because I like reading on the rug and working with the snails and Spike (the class pet rabbit).

Isabel: Ian, what's your top center? . . . Because you haven't gone to Lego.

Ian: (Quickly) Yes, I have.

Isabel: Not a lot.

Ian: Sand.

Isabel: Yeah, you do a lot of measuring of the sand and weighing it, filling up the bottles. Alan, top center?

Alan: Um, blocks. Because I like building.

Immediately, Breanna and Sue's responses indicate that Isabel has asked a ridiculous and obvious question. Clearly, Lego is considered a "boy" center in this classroom. Isabel's reaction is one of surprise. Even a teacher who is conscious of gender can misread the gender terrain of her classroom. Ian's quick and defensive reply to Isabel's observation that he has not gone to Lego supports the idea that not only is Lego for the boys, but it holds power and prestige. These reactions, from both boys and girls, show how the kindergarten curriculum is gendered. Some learning activities, such as Lego, are connected to hegemonic masculinity and influence gender norms and differences in the classroom. At the same time, though, Madison is one child who is able to cross that gender boundary and successfully play in a masculinized center.

As the conversation continued, more understandings about the genderedness of the curriculum were disclosed.

Isabel: Top center for girls, which do you think for girls? Anne.

Anne: Dramatic play.

Sophie: Paper work

Nancy: Dramatic play.

Sue: I have a lot of them but one of my favorites is um . . . discovery table.

Charmaine: Dramatic play.

Kelly: Block building.

Isabel: You know in some kindergartens girls never go to blocks? I have friends who teach kindergarten and none of their girls go to blocks. And when the teachers say to them, "Girls, why don't you get in there and build something with the blocks?" the girls say, "Blocks are a boy thing." Do you think blocks are a boy thing?

Class: **No!**

Isabel: Do you know that in some kindergartens, girls don't ever go to Lego? And sometimes the teacher says, "Girls, you really have to challenge yourself and go to those Lego." And the girls say that Lego are a boy thing. Do you think that Lego are a boy thing?

Class: (More yesses than nos.)

Isabel: (Looks over at me with a surprised expression on her face) And did you know that in some kindergartens, boys never go to dramatic play and they say, "Boys, there are things you can do in dramatic play." And the boys say, "Dramatic play is a girl thing." Do you think dramatic play is a girl thing?

Class: **No!**

Isabel: And when I show my friends pictures of this kindergarten where boys and girls do lots of things, they think it is strange. And do you know what I say? I tell them that **my** students love a challenge. **My** students can think with their very own minds, and they think of wonderful things to do no matter where they are. Hot stuff, you guys. That's why Mindy is looking at our class, because we're some hot stuff students//

Alan: //Isabel, what time is lunch?

Isabel: Yes, Alan, it's almost time for lunch, enough with the political speech. (To me) I hope that was okay for you. We aim to please. Living in the contradiction. I love that they can do this. The ambiguity is fabulous.

Isabel chooses to focus the remainder of the discussion on the centers that girls prefer and the ambiguities found with the gendering of learning centers. Drawing from her own experience as an early childhood teacher, Isabel shares the assumptions that some teachers have about blocks being for boys and the dramatic play area being for girls. In doing so, Isabel links the micropolitics of the classroom to the wider community. Collectively, the class agrees that their block and dramatic play centers are not gendered. In fact, their certainty shows how discourses change over time and are shaped by local phenomena. This indicates that change is possible and that what teachers do in their classrooms does matter. However, this conversation still holds a few surprises for Isabel. When the class disagrees about whether or not Lego is considered a "boy thing," Isabel's facial expression reveals that this is a new discovery for her. Later that afternoon, while we debriefed about this large group discussion, Isabel said, "I really was surprised that they all didn't say that Lego was for both girls and boys. I don't know what to make of that. But it is very interesting." Again, the children in this class show that they do know about the complex workings of gender discourses in their classroom.

For Isabel, the aim of this large group discussion is about confronting children with contradictory beliefs about gender as they occur in the children's daily lives. This example discloses the ways in which children understand gender and how this impacts the curriculum. First, the part that Madison plays in promoting gender equity is brought to the attention of the entire class. In doing so, other ways of being a girl are presented for the class to ponder. Second, the ways that society sees learning as gendered are raised and then disputed by class members. Third, how the boys are coping with gender is brought to the forefront of the discussion.

Isabel conducts this large group discussion because gender and equity, rather than child development, drives her practice. Instead of noticing the developmental stages of children's play, she picks up on the ways in which they are doing gender and accessing gender discourses. This then informs the large group discussions she holds. Also, by highlighting Madison's gender work, she is not only valuing the risks that Madison takes as she crosses a range of gender borders, but also providing opportunities for the entire class to see other ways of being a girl.

These gender issues do not remain exclusively at the circle. The next week I overheard Madison, Sue, Keith, and Alan having an intense discussion in line about the girls taking over Lego. Madison explained, "It **is** fair for Lego to be all girls, because some girls in this class never want to go when the boys are there. Besides it's fun to be all girls." Madison's comment confirms the negative experiences that some girls have when playing together with boys at the block center (MacNaughton, 2000). Madison's comments show that she is not trying to be a substitute boy when playing Lego. Instead, she likes girls and feels like one too.

Taking Action

Madison's interest in gender equity did not occur just within the confines of the kindergarten classroom. Additionally, she widened her equity interests to the broader community when she wrote a letter to the Lego company requesting more female Lego action figures. One day, Madison asked Isabel why there were not many girl Lego characters at table toys and requested that more get added to this center. As a result, Isabel went to purchase more female Lego action figures, only to discover that each Lego set contains only one female Lego action figure to every four male action figures. Concerned about the inequitable quantities of female action figures available within each set and the messages that are being sent to the children who played with Lego in her classroom, Isabel wrote a letter to the consumer affairs department of the Lego company inquiring about this issue. In response to her letter, the company claimed that these sets contain "gender-neutral" figures. Isabel brought this issue up with the class during morning meeting. Later, Madison said that she also wanted to write and complain to Lego. That afternoon, during writing workshop, Madison started writing her letter. The next morning she showed the following completed letter to Isabel.

> Dear Lego People,
>
> I am in kindergarten at PS 99 and I love to play with the Legos. We need more "Girl Legos" for our playtimes. Please send me some at the above address and I will bring them to school. Thank you.
>
> Sincerely,
> Madison

Madison's letter was mailed to the company, and she too received a reply in which the company claimed that its sets contained gender-neutral figures. The company also sent Madison complimentary "female-designed elements" (i.e., pink Lego blocks and Lego faces that had red lips and eyelashes) to include in the Lego at school. Later that week, Isabel addressed this issue again during meeting time and with their second- and third-grade story partners. After highlighting Madison's attempts to alter the gender discourses in the classroom, she asked the older story partners if they ever experienced similar kinds of gender inequity in their lives. Several of the girls shared how the video games they played were always made with mostly boy characters and the only girl characters were "really lame." Most children have a sense of what is fair or unfair. For Madison, this went further. Though she is a girl who likes Lego, her worldview is represented by the older girls and their experiences with video games.

Gender Bending

Not only does Madison challenge gender norms by choosing to play with Lego, but she also does so by deciding to play nonfemale characters, which I call gender bending. As a gender bender, Madison sometimes pretends to be a boy when playing at the dramatic play center. Sometimes I noticed Madison walking around the center with both fists clenched tight, showing off her muscles, talking in a deep voice, lifting heavy objects while grunting, getting into karate fights, and rescuing girls and babies from raging fires.

Exploring Power

One day during center time I watch Madison enter the dramatic play area, where she immediately tells Anne, "I'm a boy. Okay?" Anne simply nods and continues talking into the telephone. Madison then spends over 20 minutes constructing her room out of blocks, including a raised bed. While building her bed, she often states, using a loud, deep voice, "I'm a boy and I am building my own bed." Both Anne and Liam look quietly at Madison and then resume playing. Later Madison has a discussion with Anne.

Madison: (Enters through the doorway she has built, on her knees, with markers, tape, and construction paper) Mom, stop messing up my bed! That's my bed, that I built. It's sleep time.

Anne: (Pulls a long necklace and bracelet out of a jewelry box, holding them up in the air and swinging them back and forth) I bought this . . .for a present for y::o::u.

Madison: Yuck! (Grabs the jewelry out of Anne's hand and throws the bracelet into the kitchen area) I'm not a girl. I am **not** a girl! These are girl things and I don't wear them. (Turns and walks away. She returns after Anne leaves her bedroom.) Oh, I need to make my bed. (Takes a scarf and drapes it over her bed. Folds another scarf into a pillow.)

This exchange between Madison and Anne shows how young children consciously explore gendered power relationships. While pretending to be a boy, Madison experiences power. She is also contesting her gender when she exclaims that she is not a girl. By throwing the bracelets into the kitchen area and saying "yuck," she is marginalizing a particular form of femininity. Although Madison might be experiencing power in her play as she pretends to be a boy, Anne is not. This moment contradicts the literature highlighting the power that some girls find when accessing the storylines of mom and domesticity through their play (i.e., MacNaughton, 1994; Walkerdine, 1990). In this case, Anne is not experiencing power as the mother. As the mom, Anne is powerless and unable to repair the tearing of the heterosexual matrix that Madison's gender bending causes.

Liam: (Steps over the doorway, causing it to fall. Sits on the floor in the kitchen.)

Madison: I need some tape. (Begins fixing the doorway)

Anne: (Picking up things in the kitchen.) (To Liam) You better hurry up, Dad's coming home.

Liam: I'm only the brother.

Madison: (Drops something on the floor near Liam) Here, featherbrain. (Goes back into her room) I want to call my brother featherbrain because he's such a feather! (Leaning over the wall) Featherbrain brother, featherbrain!

Anne: (Cleaning up the kitchen) Don't make a mess in this
            house.

Madison: (Takes a scarf and puts it around her waist, then takes it
            off) Belts, belts go in here. (Puts the scarf in her drawer)
            Some more belts, belts. (With party dresses gathered in
            her arms) *I have no dresses, I am not a girl. **M:o:m!***
            Why are your old dresses in my room? I hate these!
            (Drops the dresses on the other side of the wall she built)
            I have to clean up this room. Put those somewhere. Take
            this, Mom. (Hands Anne a basket) Your slipper, Mom.
            (Throws it to Anne) Another shirt . . . shirts, belts . . . I
            got nothing except boy stuff. A shirt . . . these are shirts
            . . . (Continues to straighten her room) My belt. Mom,
            I'm making my room very clean. (Lifts a large hollow
            block over the wall) Here, Mom, Mom . . . Take this!
            Mom! . . . Come on, take this. That's our door, Mom.
            (Picks up a flowery scarf and puts it around her waist and
            quickly takes it off, adopts a disgusted voice) *Mom's
            skirt, ugh.* Mom (throwing the scarf over the wall),
            here's your skirt! Here's your shoe (throws it over the
            wall), stockings (throws them over the wall), Mom's
            shoes (throws them over the wall). (To Liam) Your
            room's messy! Mom, your shoe (dropping it over the wall
            to where Anne is cleaning in the kitchen) . . . I found it
            on my radiator! Here's a spoon and some grapes. Now it's
            sleep time. (Madison gets ready for bed, lies down, and
            covers herself with a scarf.)

Madison is doing more than just disregarding femininity. She is also
trying to achieve a complex performance of masculinity with its relationship to maternal power, sibling rivalry, and clothing style.

Madison: (Pointing from her bed at Liam, who has come to watch
            her) Get out of here, Liam! I'm in the attic. You can't get
            all the way to the ceiling and get me. (Gets up from bed.)
            Want some scarves? (Hands him a few scarves) Now,
            that's all the scarves you get! I'm going back to rest. (Liam
            turns and walks away)

Anne: (From the other side of the wall) Are you okay in there,
            darling?

Madison: I think I need a rest. (Lies down)

Anne: Don't make a mess.

Madison: I won't make a mess after a hard day. (Goes to sleep and quickly wakes up.) It's tomorrow. It's karate day!

Anne: (Comes over to the room) Son?

Madison: What? (Takes a scarf and wraps it around her waist, then begins singing) I have to get ready for karate. I'm getting ready for karate. Mom, I'm getting ready for karate. (Begins to do karate moves, accompanied by punching noises) You can't see me, Liam, I'm in my room. (She takes the scarf off, leaves dramatic play, and goes to the snack table)

This final section of Liam, Anne, and Madison's play reiterates how children use their understandings of hegemonic masculinity to marginalize other forms of gender. For instance, after breaking the doorway, Liam reminds everyone he's just the brother, rather than the dad. In doing this, Liam has taken himself out of the heterosexual matrix. I would argue that Liam is choosing to embody a less dominant form of masculinity as he takes on jobs and actions not considered cool or mach such as cooking and cleaning. In relation to Madison, Liam is marginalized while she fixes the doorway. Under the heterosexual matrix, boys are supposed to fix things. Liam also chooses to ignore Madison's name-calling, which would often not be tolerated by some boys, who might respond with physical violence. Madison's gender identity is important to her, and this is seen when Madison reminds Anne that she is not a girl and when she shows disgust when finding her mother's feminine items. While getting ready for karate, an odd moment occurs between Madison and Liam; as Madison performs hegemonic masculinity for Liam, he quietly watches. It is odd because a female is teaching a male about the discourse of hegemonic masculinity.

Although hegemonic masculinity marginalizes both Anne and Liam throughout this episode, they both support Madison's gender bending. Neither tells Madison that she is not allowed to be a boy. Instead they reinforce her play by straightening rooms and complimenting the construction. When Anne calls Madison "son," she is supporting Madison's choice to bend the gender rules, and she might be enjoying the vicarious pleasure of Madison being a boy. For the most part, Liam and Anne both watch quietly as Madison performs hegemonic masculinity.

Madison's gender bending can also be interpreted as a different form of femininity that offers power and access to a new set of discourses. Discourses are neither static nor permanent. By performing gender, as a girl and in very different ways, Madison is enlarging the possibilities for all of her classmates. She is challenging the power of the heterosexual matrix by making new spaces within it. Furthermore, these new spaces might entail lesbian possibilities if Madison is desired by other girls.

Sharing Views

While Madison was gender bending, I was sitting at the snack table talking to Keith, Katy, Kelly, Breanna, and Sue. When Madison joined our conversation, I asked the following:

Mindy: Madison, what do you like to play when you go to the dramatic play center?

Madison: Well, I like to play house . . . and I pretend that I'm the brother . . . the older brother.

Mindy: But you're a girl?

Madison: But I hate being a girl.

Mindy: Why?

Madison: Because I just hate being . . . (looks away)

Penny: //But girl is **much more** prettier. (looking at Madison, with a confused look on her face)

Madison: I just hate being prettier.

Mindy: Why?

Madison: Because I just hate it.

Mindy: Penny, would you ever consider playing a boy?

Penny: No, no, no, no (shaking head).

Mindy: Why not?

Penny: Because I don't like boys. I don't want to be a boy.

Mindy: Why do you play being a boy, Madison, why do you like playing being a boy? What kind of things do you do that a girl couldn't do?

Madison: Because it's just better. I can be, um, be stronger and do more things. You get to do more stuff, be cool, and it's easier (shrugging).

Mindy: So in your dramatic play, what would you do that would be stronger?

Madison: Pick up something that is very heavy.

Mindy: What other things would you be if you were a boy, playing a boy?

Madison: I don't know . . . karate. I could do karate and fight.

Madison's desire to gender bend at dramatic play is based on her dislike of emphasized femininity and the limitations that the current gender discourses impose. Instead of accepting femininity as it is currently understood, she is creating new feminine discourses that are liberating. When Madison explains that being a boy is better and easier than being a girl, she understands the struggle to either be powerful or conform. Often, it is easier and more acceptable to conform to current, mainstream ways of being either a girl or a boy. With this in mind, it is necessary to think about the hard and risky gender work Madison explores. Children such as Madison need support in their efforts at resisting conventional ways of being gendered.

However, Penny knows the rules for being a girl, in which a high value is placed on beauty. As we saw in the previous chapter, Penny is often silent, but in this case she believes that being a beautiful girl is important enough to speak up. Madison and Penny's understandings of what it means to be a girl are based on different discourses, which in this case are competing.

Undermining Heterosexuality

Although Madison was only observed gender bending in dramatic play, she did not perform masculinity exclusively as a teenage boy. As the following video data show, Madison also sometimes pretends to be a (male) dog.

Katy, Kelly, Madison, and Theresa are playing in dramatic play. Katy is the mother, Kelly and Theresa are sisters, and Madison is a dog. Katy and Kelly are at the pet shop buying a puppy.

Kelly: (Petting Madison) I want to buy this little doggy . . . Mommy, Mother . . . Look at the puppy.

Katy: (Bending down and begins petting) A show puppy!

Madison: No, I'm just a little boy puppy///

Katy: //No, pretend you're a show champion. Do you know what a show champion is? It's a really fun dog, they play a lot//

Madison: //No, I want to be a puppy Dalmatian, a **boy** puppy Dalmatian.

Katy: How about a show champion puppy Dalmatian?

Kelly: She just wants to be a puppy Dalmatian. (They leave the pet store with their new puppy and bring the puppy home)

.

.

.

Katy: Who's gonna be the husband?

Theresa: No one, there aren't any boys.

Kelly is standing on top of some blocks and reaches down to Madison, who is on the floor licking and barking. Madison then stands up and faces Katy.

Madison: Pretend, Katy, Katy. Pretend you thought that Kelly was just up in her room . . . but she was trapped, but I, pretend that I save Kelly. Pretend she gets stuck upstairs and there's a fire, and she got trapped and I told you. I come and bark and you know what I'm saying. First I go upstairs. (Begins barking)

Pretending to be the dog is a familiar role in the dramatic play center. However, it is a role that traditionally does not have a lot of power, as it is usually given to the boys and controlled by Mom. Madison's "Lassie" version of power is a better way to be a rescuer, rather than pretending to be the hegemonic male. As a dog, Madison still gets to experience power as she rescues others, but unlike hegemonic masculinity, she is not marginalizing others. Since romance is not involved in the relationships that Madison has with others while pretending to be a dog, this play undercuts the heterosexual matrix. As a dog, Madison gets to be happy as she barks, licks, and is warmly loved. Pretending to be a male dog is not done unconsciously. Madison likes to experience power but is unhappy with the limited scripts. As a dog, she has carved out a script that feels right for her. If Madison's play fails to reinforce the heterosexual matrix, then some children may find this uncomfortable, particularly Alan, who likes the power he is able to access through heterosexual discourses.

Knowing the Risks

Madison's classmates did not seem bothered by her gender bending, and I never saw anyone actively preventing her from performing masculine discourses. Alan rarely played with Madison, and I believe that this is because her play might make him feel uncomfortable. Attempting to understand more about gender bending and the counterdiscourses these scripts provide, I engaged Madison and a group of girls (Breanna, Anne, Penny, Theresa, and Amy) in a discussion about gender during center time, when we were sitting at a table in the hall and painting bracelets.

Madison: I like boys, the way they dress. I wear boy shoes, he wears girl shoes. You know those black shoes that I have?

Mindy: Yeah. The Batman shoes?

Madison: No, they're not Batman.

Mindy: Remember those Batman shoes you used to wear in the beginning of the year?

Madison: Oh yeah.

Mindy: Are those girls' or boys' shoes?

Madison: Boys'.

Breanna: Boys'.

Mindy: So you had to buy boy shoes?

Madison: No, I like them. I like to be a boy//.

Breanna: I like to be boys.

Mindy: You do? Why?

Theresa: I like to be a girl (tapping my arm).

Madison: Because.

Breanna: Because//

Madison: //Because I love boys and because I love boy stuff//

Breanna: Madison, she's talking to me. Because they're fancy.

Mindy: Boys are? How?

Breanna: Because//

Madison: //'Cause boys have cooler stuff.

Breanna: I like to be cool.

Madison: And you know why? Because Mindy like, um, see, how about if you were a girl and I was just born then, I was just born to be to be like a boy?

Mindy: So, do you think about that a lot?

Breanna: Some boys are like girls.

Madison: Yes. And it is hard for them

This conversation shows both Madison and Breanna explaining gender bending. Like Madison, Breanna understands that boys have access to power, and she likes experiencing this. Madison also understands the cultural capital that certain forms of masculinity have in society. This is evident in the way that Madison talks about her Batman shoes, making sure that I understood the difference between *having* to buy and *wanting* to buy these shoes. Again, Madison gets the subtleties of gender and how gender discourses work. Madison is conscious of her gender choices and knows that moving beyond particular ways of being a girl is full of risks. As the conversation continues, both Madison and Breanna struggle to articulate the ways that they attempt to move beyond the heterosexual matrix in their everyday lives.

Mindy: Are there some girls who like to do that?

Anne: Maybe.

Breanna: Yes.

Madison: Yes.

Mindy: Like who?

Madison: Only girls that think they're, they're, that want to be a boy, like me and Breanna.

Mindy: Who else?

Madison: And that's it.

Mindy: Liza?

Madison: Liza too.

Breanna: She may be a girl but I think she acts like a boy.

Madison: Maybe we are girls, right? When I went to the bathroom I saw a boy part right on my private part. So I think I'm a boy. I think I was just imagining it. Because my eyes were closed.

Theresa: (Stops painting her bracelet, turns toward Madison, and then looks at me) What did she say?

Breanna: Can we hear the tape recorder?

Madison: Oooh, purple, I hate purple.

Anne: I like girl colors, because I'm a girl.

Theresa: I'm a girl also.

Madison: I like boy colors, because I'm a boy.

From this discussion, Liza is named as a third female gender bender in this class. Through her talk, Madison explains that she sometimes dreams and imagines herself to have a boy part, a penis. Theresa reacts to her comment in shock and disbelief as she stops painting her bracelet, turns her body toward Madison, and inquires out loud about Madison's statement. Madison takes a big risk here by explaining to the table her dissatisfaction about being a girl and her queer desires. The girls at the table are uncomfortable with Madison's comments, as they ignore what is said. I believe that Madison knows that she has pushed the envelope, possibly going too far, so she changes the direction of the conversation to focus on colors rather than her gender desires.

Playing the Heterosexual Game

Conversations with Madison and observations of her talk and actions in the classroom indicate how she is aware of the politics of gender, understanding the many ways that heterosexual norms work to marginalize both boys and girls. Although Madison rarely exhibits overt forms of femininity, this section discloses how she uses femininity strategically to access power.

Madison was observed performing various forms of femininity. In doing so, the contradictory and competing features of her gender identities becomes apparent to me and the other children in the classroom. At times, she accessed transgressive gender discourses, positioning herself in relation to hegemonic masculinity (Weedon, 1997). The following events occurred outside, while the children were playing at a nearby park.

> As spring unfolds, the class takes advantage of the warm afternoons and heads for the local park to have outdoor play and enjoy a picnic lunch. It is sunny, warm, and the park is full of people and activities. Children of various ages and ethnicities are running, laughing, and playing in the park. I situate myself near a wooden climbing structure, consisting of two hanging ropes for climbing and swinging. These ropes are surrounded on both sides by two wooden platforms, approximately four feet in height. Children climb the platforms in order to grab the rope and then swing back and forth. While one child swings, others wait on the platform for their turn. Often children give a push to the person on the rope, making for a longer (and better) swing. There are approximately eight children swinging and waiting to swing on the ropes at any one time. When it is Madison's turn

to swing, she confidently takes hold of the rope and, without hesitating, fiercely jumps, making for a long and powerful swing. Her smile and laughter indicate that jumping and swinging on the rope are exciting.

After approximately 15 minutes of watching the swinging, I am distracted by a scuffle occurring between two children near the sand pit. As I turn around, I notice that Madison and Jake are wrestling on the ground. Jake, a feisty redheaded boy from another kindergarten class, is often in trouble for pushing and shoving during recess and therefore spends quite a bit of time on the bench in time-out. Madison seems to have made Jake pretty upset, and he is kicking her. Madison gets hurt and begins crying. As I begin to walk over and intervene, Jake runs off, leaving Madison alone in the sand. Madison stops crying and quickly runs off.

Thirty minutes later, I notice Kelly organizing a system of rules for taking turns on the ropes. Jake arrives, pushing himself in front of Kelly, and begins telling everyone his new rules for taking turns. Scott, a boy from another kindergarten class, is handed the rope and begins swinging. Madison is now standing on the platform. She stretches her hand out toward Scott, smiling at him and saying, *"Sc:o:tt, can you give it to me? . . . I'll marry you . . . . . . I'll marry you if you give it to me!"* Scott quickly gets off the rope, handing it to Madison. As Scott jumps down from the platform, Jake leaps after him, grabbing his shirt. Scott yells, "I want her to marry me!" Jake replies, "*No!* I want her to marry me!" A fight starts as they begin grabbing and punching each other. Now Scott is crying, while Jake quickly looks around the playground before deciding to leave. I look back at the ropes to find Madison swinging, oblivious to the boys' fight.

This example with the rope shows how Madison plays the heterosexual game and uses a range of strategies to gain access to the rope. She positions herself in relation to Scott, by using her smile, voice, and the promise of marriage in exchange for the rope. She is exchanging a particular feminine performance for a chance to swing on the rope! Is Madison simply complying with a set of gender norms, or is she strategically using her knowledge of heterosexual discourses to gain power? Madison's actions show that she is clearly not diminished by this play. Instead, she gets what she wants as well as incidentally confirming that she is desirable even though she actively challenges the heterosexual matrix.

Expanding "Girldom"

Madison bravely takes risks in her daily gender work, and in doing so, she expands what it means to be a girl. She confidently utilizes her knowledge about gender discourses and the heterosexual matrix to be the kind of girl she wants to be. This is seen in the ways that she challenges gender norms, through crossing gender boundaries, discussions with classmates, and playing at Lego. For Madison, crossing gender boundaries in her play allows her to experience another gender discourse in which she can position herself in more powerful ways. As a result, her play functions as a counterdiscourse, providing a space for Madison to resist conventional notions of femininity and expanding the possibilities for other children.

What becomes evident in this chapter are the multiple subjectivities that Madison experiences as a girl in this classroom. By not performing a single form of femininity, Madison's gender identities are complicated, sometimes contradictory, and empowering. There are certainly more ways to be a girl than just wearing pink, playing mom, and drawing at the writing center with friends.

Implications for Researching and Teaching in Early Childhood Education

It is important that children like Madison, who expand and transcend gender norms, are supported in the classroom. Isabel does this most noticeably through large group discussions. These critical conversations are possible because Isabel recognizes and values Madison's gender work. Although Isabel supported and highlighted a variety of ways that Madison challenged gender, her gender bending was never mentioned with the entire class. The counterdiscourses that some children create while challenging gender norms might be used by teachers to have honest discussions with the class about the gains and losses that are experienced through this kind of play. For example, it would be interesting to explore when it is easiest and when it is hardest for these children to challenge gender. These discussions can support other children in generating their own counterdiscourses. Additionally, the dramatic play area might become a space in the curriculum where boys and girls can safely alter and dismantle gender discourses without being teased or bullied.

When overhearing children having important discussions about gender, as was the case when Breanna, Madison, and Penny talked about their desires and fears about transgressing girldom, teachers and researchers can affirm and support these conversations. These discussions might then lead a teacher or a researcher towards seeing possible gender coalitions (Bryson & de Castell, 1997) between children as they interact with each other during the school day. If so, teachers might consider creating opportunities for children to build these coalitions in a range of situations. In the early childhood classroom this implies that instead of having children freely choose a learning center during center time, the teacher might suggest that particular children play together because they might be more successful challenging gender norms as a group, rather than individually. This would not be done covertly. Instead, a teacher would clearly explain her reasoning to the children. For example, after noticing the ways that Sue, Katy, and Madison publicly question some of the boys' actions, Isabel could have suggested to these girls, "I am impressed with how the three of you tell the boys what you think. Not many girls can do this. I think it would be interesting if the three of you worked together on reading on the rug." Creating and supporting gender coalitions between children could also become a grouping strategy used by teachers who are interested in collective action.

Again, these strategies will not be easy for teachers, researchers, and some children. Children like Madison may not always want the ways that they choose to confront gender norms to be noticed. Teachers and researchers will need to carefully listen to children while they are inventing new pedagogies aimed at supporting the hard gender work that is currently being done in early childhood settings.

6

PENNY: THE "GOOD" GIRL

Penny is a working-class Asian American girl who positions herself in the classroom as quiet, nice, kind, and helpful. She is well behaved and most teachers would consider her a "good" girl. Like Alan, she understands gender discourses and how they work in the classroom and society. In many ways, Penny is the opposite of Alan. While Alan works hard at accessing discourses of hegemonic masculinity, Penny is just as vigilant about being a good girl. However, locating the gender work that Penny does in the classroom is challenging. Emphasized femininity is about being silent, quiet, compliant, and good. These characteristics are tough to notice because they are not visually or physically as loud as hegemonic masculinity. As part of the dominant discourse of heterosexuality, emphasized femininity appears natural and normal, making it difficult to recognize and document. Although it was hard to document Penny's talk and actions in the classroom, I was able to locate a range of ways that Penny does gender in the classroom, allowing me to discover how she uses emphasized femininity to experience power.

These common ways for girls to do gender are problematic. First, most of the girls want to be good. Second, good-girl behavior usually frees the teacher to work with the more difficult-to-manage boys. This results in girls receiving less time, less help, and fewer challenges from the teacher. Third, teachers, children, and dominant gender discourses work together, operating as a powerful system that reinforces gender norms (Sadker & Sadker, 1995). An understanding of Penny's choices for enacting emphasized femininity and what she gains from doing so might help teachers understand the roles that both they themselves and the children they teach play in maintaining gender norms.

Penny's gendered performances were easy to miss in the classroom. Unlike the efforts I had made *not* to notice Alan and his masculinity, for Penny I had to do the opposite and make intentional efforts to find her and her feminine performances. Isabel understood how Penny's identity was hard to notice and recognized Penny as a girl who is "invisible but productive." That is, although Penny might be quiet and mild-mannered, she was doing valuable and valid gender work, though this work was more difficult to notice and appreciate when compared to that of Madison or Alan. Alan's ability to use discourses of hegemonic masculinity to position himself powerfully in relation to others and Madison's confidence in engaging counterdiscourses were both ways of doing gender "loudly" when compared to Penny.

Racialized Heterosexism

Although I did not set out to document how Penny's race intersects with her gender, there are instances in which being Asian American influences the ways in which Penny embodies femininity. Knowing about this is vital if we want to move beyond stereotypical understandings of gender. In addition to being good and quiet, which are characteristics of emphasized femininity, they are also attributes of the "model minority" stereotype of Asian American students (Lee, 1996). Although heterosexism in Asian American communities is similar to that in mainstream society, it has an additional racialized dimension. Drawing from his own experiences as a queer Asian American male, Kumashiro (1999) discusses how Asian American society assigns racial markers to different sexual orientations. He goes on to say, "In particular, the 'traditional Asian values' of getting married, having children, and passing down the family name, imply that being a virtuous or real Asian American requires . . . the performance of heterosexuality"

(p. 67). For Asian Americans, heterosexuality is racialized, and it is an Asian value. This racialized heterosexism adds another layer of complexity to Penny, how she does gender in the classroom, and how her gender performances are understood.

Doing Emphasized Femininity Correctly

Penny is an only child and does not live with her mother or father. Instead, she lives with a large extended family, consisting of grandparents, aunts, and uncles. Penny's two aunts escort her to and from school and often talk to Isabel about their niece's educational needs. Although Penny wears both pants and dresses to school, she always looks like a girly girl. Her clothes are usually pink or pastel in color and are decorated with pictures of kittens, flowers, or bears. A bracelet, necklace, or pair of earrings completes her fashion style and feminine look. Unlike Madison's unkempt hairstyle, Penny's shoulder-length black hair is always neatly brushed and sometimes pulled back with a matching hair ribbon or barrette. The ways in which Penny and Madison care about their appearance are an example of how different cultures have different expectations for how girls should look and present themselves in public.

Not only does Penny portray emphasized femininity through her choice of fashion, but she also does this in the work that she produces in school. In art class, children made a series of self-portraits. These projects include a photograph of the child, a drawing done by the child, and a collage the child created of him- or herself. In Penny's three-part project, she is photographed working at paper work and is pictured smiling while sitting at a messy table among assorted paper, markers, glue, and scissors. Her drawing displays three attributes that are often considered feminine in society: first, she chose a light pink piece of paper to draw on; second, she drew herself with long, curly eyelashes; third, the lips that she has drawn are enormous and red, taking up most of her face. Finally, her collage contains an oversized cut-out heart, which she glued onto her body. Penny clearly has definite ideas about what femininity means, as seen through her art project.

Penny likes, admires, and desires feminine items. For example, Penny was impressed with the Barbie cake that Valerie brought to school for her birthday celebration. A real Barbie doll was used for the body, and her skirt was made of cake and pink icing, decorated with a pattern of flowers. As children slowly entered the classroom and began sitting on the rug, Penny walked up to me, smiling and pointing to the Barbie cake while exclaiming, "**Look!** We get to have that. She is so:oo:oo pretty!" As children started choosing which learning center they would go to during center time, Penny was unable to take her eyes off the Barbie cake. She sat on the rug, mesmerized, until she was the only child left there.

Penny has several friends in the classroom. No one seems to mind being paired up with her as a partner, and there is no moaning or groaning when she invites someone to be her line partner. In terms of the heterosexual matrix, Penny's niceness is a direct consequence of doing emphasized femininity correctly. As a result, Penny is the perfect companion. She would rather play with girls than boys and would probably not pick a boy to be her line partner unless she had to. Again, Penny is acting in ways considered appropriate and normal for young girls.

Although Penny is friendly with all of the girls in the classroom, she shares a special friendship with Charmaine, Nancy, and Anne, three working-class girls of color. I often saw these four girls playing together at recess, sharing lunch, or sitting side by side on the rug in the front row for morning meeting and story time. Collectively, they liked being good girls and were often seen regulating one another's behaviors. One afternoon I overheard Penny snap at Charmaine, "You can't do that, it's not right . . . you're going to get in trouble." Their friendship and connectedness were most visible on the rug as they huddled together whispering and giggling. Rarely did I see them sitting apart or near the back of the rug; instead they stayed close together and near Isabel.

Isabel understands how Penny's gender and race intersect and position her in the classroom. When discussing how Penny does her identity work in the classroom, Isabel explains, "Penny is one of four children who live, work, and play within the margins of this classroom." Penny takes a backseat during large group discussions. For example, when attempting to answer a question in class, Penny raises her hand quietly, without calling out or waving her hand wildly, like some of her classmates. Since Penny rarely draws attention to herself, it is unlikely that she will volunteer for work share. Therefore, like most quiet and good girls, Penny's academic achievements and gender work go unnoticed. Knowing this, Isabel changes Penny's powerlessness by providing opportunities for her to participate in work share that support her gendered and cultural ways. For example, Isabel asked Penny to share the work she did during center time with a group of friends, rather than by herself.

Although Penny is well-behaved and congenial in the classroom, it was evident from my observations that she does not particularly like Keith, the only African American boy in the class, and discreetly avoids him during the school day. She accomplishes this by using strategies that would not single her out as being impolite. For example, I observed Penny quietly moving her body away from Keith, rather than remaining beside him on the rug. Another day, while standing in line for music, Penny noticed that Keith was directly behind her. She looked at her line partner, Charmaine, and whispered, "We need to move." Penny then gently pulled Charmaine away from Keith, and they moved to the end of the line. Penny could have pushed Keith, called him a name, or sternly told him to get away from her. However, all of these actions have the potential of singling Penny out, positioning her as rude or impolite. When asked what she does not like about school, Penny answered, "I do not like Keith because he speaks too loud and doesn't listen to Isabel." By staying away from Keith, Penny avoids corruption and being labeled as bad. Also, if hegemonic masculinity is based on whiteness and being middle-class, then Penny is drawing on discourses of race and knows that Keith is not a suitable partner within the heterosexual matrix. This is an interesting moment because it illuminates how Keith is situated within a racialized discourse. Connolly's (1998) work on racism, culture, and identity shows how the racialized discourses of black boys in the early childhood context position boys such as Keith as troublesome. Penny seems to know this and to see Keith's corruption as race-based.

Although Penny is a strong student academically and enjoys reading, drawing, and writing, these characteristics only reinforce the "model minority" stereotype that Asian Americans are good students (Lee, 1996). Penny likes all parts of the school day, especially center time.

She enjoys going to a range of centers and during center time can be found busily working at the writing table, the discovery center, the reading area on the rug, or the blocks, but always with a friend. Even though Penny is observed playing at blocks, in the culture of this classroom they are not considered a masculine center.

Penny values her friendships and would rather play with or near friends at a learning center than work alone. One day during center time, I noticed Penny and Nancy playing at the dollhouse. Out of ten learning centers in the classroom, the children consider the dollhouse to be the most "girly" center, and my observations reveal that the boys rarely visit here. I mentioned to Penny and Nancy that some of the girls had told me that the dollhouse was a boring center, and I was curious if they agreed. Penny replied, "No, we are together," pointing back and forth between herself and Nancy. "If we have two, that means the dollhouse is not boring. If we have only one, then it is boring." Unlike Alan, who values working independently, Penny prefers working with friends. One way that Penny confirms her identity as a girl is through the acceptance of others, and this is accomplished by doing her gender "right" as she plays at the appropriate centers and with groups of girls. Penny's need for quiet acceptance is the flip side of Alan's desire for public recognition. Not only does this quiet acceptance reinforce the gendered notion that females remain in the private sphere, whereas males belong in the public domain, but these ideas also position masculinity and femininity in a binary. Penny's wish to work with others at a learning center is different from Madison's contentment at playing alone with materials. This preference illuminates the different ways that Madison and Penny enact femininity in the classroom.

Another difference found between Madison and Penny is in the choices they make during center time. The table toy center, where the Lego materials are located, is the only learning center that Penny does not frequently visit. In the middle of the school year, I had a conversation with Madison about who liked playing with Lego in her class. Madison explained how some children "tried" Lego, while others "did" it, distinguishing between the two kinds of engagement that children have with Lego. When I inquired about Penny, Madison replied, "Trying, because she's never been here before." From this conversation and the time of the school year, it is implied that after being in school for approximately six months, Penny has yet to play with or "do" Lego.

It is interesting how the children are aware of the play preferences of their classmates. When Penny chose to give the table toy center a try and play with Lego, her actions were noteworthy and included in a Friday Memory Web. Revisiting the twenty Memory Webs that I collected revealed that boys were never recognized by their peers for playing at a feminized learning center, such as the dollhouse. And yet Penny's "try" at Lego was significant because this masculinized learning center, as revealed in a previous class discussion about the genderedness of the centers, holds power and prestige. Like the incident with the rope in physical education class, children avoid shameful gender slumming, but they acknowledge the opposite.

Penny frequently goes to the dramatic play center with friends. Playing house is a common story line performed here. When playing house, the task of negotiating various roles is usually done before children begin enacting the parts of mother, daughter, baby, or sister. As several studies of young children's play have shown, domesticity and being mom is a desired and powerful role for the girls (i.e., MacNaughton, 1994; Walkerdine, 1990). One morning I observed Penny and Charmaine arguing over who would be the mom. Penny insisted that families only have one mom. With both hands placed on her hips, she said to Charmaine, "Listen, we can only have one mom. That is how a family is!" This is a familiar assertion, but striking here given how little resemblance it bears to Penny's experience of family, in which she has several "moms." Penny noticed that I was sitting on the floor beside dramatic play and quickly approached me, saying, "Mindy, tell Charmaine that we can only have one mom . . . people don't have two moms." I reply, "Well, not all families have just one mom. Lucinda [another kindergartner] has two moms, and I have a friend who has two moms. So I think it would be okay for you to both be moms." Penny did not respond and walked back to the dramatic play area. Silence is a way of being in the classroom for Penny, and her silence makes it difficult to know what she is thinking. It was not until the following week that the topic of having two moms surfaced again, when I saw Penny quietly whispering to Katy the idea of having a family with two moms while playing at the dramatic play area.

It is center time, and Penny, Theresa, Katy, and Ian are playing in dramatic play. Katy and Theresa have been getting dressed for Katy's wedding. Penny has not been involved in their play. Instead she is seated on a block, quietly reading a book. Ian is playing with the computer keyboard by himself.

Theresa: (Walks over to Penny, tapping her with her foot) Where are my shoes?

Penny: (Shrugs, gets up from the block, and walks up to Katy, watching her fix a veil on top of her head) Pretend I'm your mom, okay?

Katy: No, no, Theresa's the mother.

Penny: (Lowering her voice while looking down at the floor) *No, pretend there's two moms.*

Katy: And I'm the auntie, so I'm getting married . . . How about I adopt you, how about that?

Penny: Okay. (Turns and walks away)

Katy: Theresa, I adopted Penny . . . a long time ago. (Theresa gets up from the block and walks toward Katy. Katy ties a scarf around and over her veil.) Pretend that Penny's a little girl and I took her.

Theresa: (Nods) Why do you always get to be the bride?

Katy: Because we worked it out. Now I'm the bride . . . and you're the mother. (At this point Penny leaves the dramatic play center)

Someone working from a socialization perspective might believe that Penny's suggestion of having two moms is evidence of her acceptance of lesbian families, a direct result of my comment earlier in the week. However, I believe that this is not the case. Instead of worrying about if Penny understands lesbianism, I am more interested in the ways she uses her knowledge of the power of mom, and I think she likes having twice as much chance of being mom. Also, Penny's cautious actions while suggesting that there are two moms—she inclines her head toward the floor and lowers her voice—shows that this is a risky idea. Like Madison, she too understands heteronormativity, and her suggestion could have been violently shut down. Instead, she is ignored, and as a result, Penny, like a good girl, quietly leaves the dramatic play center, rather than disrupt the status quo. Interestingly, as Penny leaves the center, Katy and Theresa are negotiating among themselves about being the mother and the bride, two forms of femininity that potentially hold powerful positions, but with the bride being more glamorous.

Under the Microscope

At first glance, Penny appears to be a "good" girl, performing femininity that closely follows society's expectations of how young Asian girls look and act. She adorns herself with the "right" accessories for young girls and acts and plays in the "right" ways. Penny was never witnessed coming to school dressed in provocative or sexy clothes, because wearing such clothes is not part of being silent or good. Emphasized femininity is expressed in several ways in this classroom. Most evident are the girly girls, whose behavior can be thought of as a more silent way of being a girl when compared to the cool girls, whose behaviors enable girls to hold a bit more power and speech. As a good girl, Penny listens to Isabel, follows the classroom rules, and is nice to her classmates. Her femininity appears natural and uncomplicated, because this is what we expect to see and hear.

As an Asian American girl, Penny's femininity interacts with and is complicated by her cultural background. How Penny practices these ways of being a girl when others are not watching discloses that she is aware of gender discourses and knows how to use them. For example, when it was time for writing workshop, I joined Penny, Nancy, Laura, Cheng, James, and Ian's table, where James was drawing with a green marker.

Penny: (Looking toward James) *Ja::mes,* can I borrow that green marker?

James: No.

Penny: (Smiling, batting eyelashes, and tilting her head slightly forward) *Pl:ea:se, just for a second?*

James: Do you want me to get you another one?

Penny: Well, okay. (James gets up and goes to get Penny another green marker)

This exchange between Penny and James is another example of how gender is created relationally. Assuming that discourses of gender are always circulating, Penny is using her knowledge of emphasized femininity to obtain the green marker. By smiling, tilting her head toward the floor, moving her body closer to James, and coyly saying "James" and "please" while requesting the green marker, she is strategically using forms of femininity to charm James. And yet Penny's talk and actions might go unnoticed because they appear natural and normal for her (as an Asian American girl) to perform. Instead of just letting Penny use his marker, James leaves his work to find her another one. Penny and James are working together, rather than against each other, as they constitute themselves within the heterosexual matrix. Both of their actions and talk reinforce and maintain gender differences and gender roles. Penny has to abandon silence to achieve this but does so in a safe way, by remaining within the discourse of emphasized femininity.

Another way that Penny's cultural identity reinforces gender norms is found in the way that Alan was unable to accept Penny's ability to successfully climb the rope in physical education. Referring back to the conversation I had with Alan about the strong girls in his classroom reveals Penny's invisibility.

Mindy: Who are the three strongest girls?

Alan: Nobody. (He is looking directly at me and his voice and facial expression indicate that I have asked a ridiculous question)

Mindy: None of the girls are strong?

Alan: (Turns away from me, shrugging)

Mindy: I saw some of those girls climbing that rope—they looked pretty strong.

Alan: It was boys. Loren is strong.

Mindy: Yeah, Loren is strong. But I also saw Breanna, Katy, and Penny climb the rope//

Alan: //because they're {inaudible}

Mindy: That doesn't mean that they're strong?

Alan: Nuh-uh. (Shakes head) If they're strong, they will have big, big, big muscles. (He bends his arm to show off his muscle, and tenses his entire body)

Mindy: And they shouldn't have big muscles?

Alan: No, they **don't**. I don't see any. (Stands up, turns away, and begins kicking the wall)

As demonstrated in the previous analysis regarding Alan's inability to "see" the girls successfully climbing the rope, Penny's achievement is invisible because of her femininity. Regardless of her actions in physical education or her success within a particular feminine gendered performance, the discourses of hegemonic masculinity position her in particular ways. Not only do these gender discourses prevent Alan from seeing Penny as capable, but I too found it difficult to see Penny and her gender work in more complicated ways.

Same Problem, Different Solutions

As we have seen, children were confronted by counterdiscourses in a variety of ways in this classroom. As will be seen in the next chapter, the following conversation portrays a struggle between Penny and Madison to articulate their own responses to the heterosexual matrix.

Madison: But I hate being a girl.

Mindy: Why?

Madison: Because I just hate being . . . (looks away)

Penny: //But girl is **much more** prettier. (looking at Madison, with a confused look on her face)?

Madison: I just hate being prettier.

Mindy: Why?

Madison: Because I just hate it.

Mindy: Penny, would you ever consider playing a boy?

Penny: No, no, no, no (shaking head).

Mindy: Why not?

Penny: Because I don't like boys. I don't want to be a boy.

Mindy: Why do you play being a boy, Madison, why do you like playing being a boy? What kind of things do you do that a girl couldn't do?

Madison: Because it's just better. I can be, um, be stronger and do more things. You get to do more stuff, be cool, and it's easier (shrugging).

Mindy: So in your dramatic play, what would you do that would be stronger?

Madison: Pick up something that is very heavy.

While sitting at the snack table and enjoying a snack, Penny's understandings about what it means to be a girl are challenged. As Madison shares her gender-bending stories, Penny's responses and facial expressions indicate that she is confused by Madison's desire to be a boy. Some children in this class, such as Breanna and Liza, appreciate Madison's attempts at challenging gender norms. However, Penny does not and resists the idea of breaking free of emphasized femininity. Penny is unable to understand why someone would not desire to play the heterosexual game.

It is important to remember the different ways that girls experience power when enacting particular forms of femininity. Penny relies on the feminine notion that beauty is highly valued and desired for girls and women as a reason for not wanting to be a boy. Although Penny does not desire to take part in gender bending, she is exposed to other ways of being gendered, which provide the possibility that she too might resist certain gender norms. Penny knows that she has this possibility, and it is an active choice not to take it up. It is just as much work to be a girly girl (possibly more), but it is work that is currently more valued within the heterosexual matrix, and that is why Penny does it.

Penny's Gendered Birthday Party

Penny turned six years old in the spring, and like most of the children in the class, Penny had a birthday party at school. Interestingly, because of the birthday party materials that Penny's Family supplied, her party provides an example of how Penny's values and beliefs about gender enter into the curriculum and how Isabel's awareness of gender influences her teaching practices.

> As I arrive in the classroom, I notice a beautiful white cake sitting on the shelf, decorated with slices of fruit. This is not the kind of cake I usually see at children's birthday parties. That is, the cake does not have a Disney character on top of it or Barbie stuck in the middle and decorated with icing. Instead, this cake looks more like a "grown-up" cake. While I am admiring the cake, Isabel explains that it is Penny's birthday and that her aunts brought the cake and a bag full of items for a birthday celebration. I peek inside the bag and discover paper cups, plates, napkins, hats, and party bags. While looking through the bag, Isabel exclaims, "Hey, Mindy, look at this." In her left hand is a pink paper plate and in her right a blue one. Taking a closer look, I notice that one set of party materials is definitely for the girls and the other set is for boys. The boys' plates, cups, and napkins are decorated with bold primary colors, including a picture of two boys wearing hard hats and driving a yellow tractor. The girls' place settings are colored in pink and pastel colors and include a picture of a pretty young girl playing dress-up. The girl is seated in front of a mirror, admiring her long blond hair. She is dressed in costume jewelry and a floppy hat. It is also apparent that she has on lipstick and blush.

For some teachers, it is a challenge when materials brought from home have sexist or violent connotations. As a result, some teachers have a rule banning these toys, such as Barbie or pretend guns, from their classroom. Additionally, when we claim to work from the child's interests, there is a dilemma when these items reinforce heterosexual norms.

> Isabel suggests that we place exactly ten boy plates and sixteen girl plates on the tables, purposely not setting enough places for the girls. We mix the place settings to have girls and boys sitting together at some of the tables. However, we also created a "boy table" at the feminized dollhouse center by placing only two boy plates at this table and we created a "girl table" by placing only six girl plates at the masculinized Lego table. Isabel said she was intending to confront the class with a gender challenge. That is, the children will have to make decisions regarding where they

sit. This has the possibility of becoming problematic and contentious because there will not be enough girl place settings for all of the girls to sit at a girl spot, forcing them to sit at a boy place setting, Isabel explains that she is interested in how the children will make their decisions to sit for the birthday celebration.

Soon the children arrive from their music class. As they walk into the classroom, they are observed admiring the set tables, making comments about the paper plates, cups, and napkins. Instead of directly going to the rug, Ian takes his time, casually walking around the tables, while looking at the various place settings. He taps Raoul on the shoulder and points to a boy plate, stating, "Look at the tractor. It's cool." Theresa abruptly stops walking and stares at the Lego table, which has all girl place settings. At first she has a puzzled look on her face, but then she slowly smiles and turns toward me, exclaiming in a high-pitched voice, "Ooooh! Pretty pink plates!" As Cheng lowers his body onto the rug he points back and forth between the "boy table," which is made up of the two boy plates at the dollhouse center, and himself and chants, "Me boy. Me boy." Cheng is working hard to get his gender right. Keith looks at Cheng and shakes his head. Almost everyone is seated on the rug, and there is quite a bit of whispering going on between children. There is a sense of excitement in the classroom. Keith has yet to find a seat on the rug and is leisurely wandering around looking at the tables. He stops to look at a boy plate and says with a smile to Dilta, the part-time female teaching assistant, "This one's for a boy."

The class is now seated in a circle, along the edge of the rug. Penny passes out the party hats. At first, the children do not put the hats on their heads. Noticing this, Isabel puts a party hat on. Children excitedly begin discussing the different hat designs with each other. I observe Ian turning to Alan, asking, "Hey, is this a boy hat?" Alan nods. As Penny passes out the rest of the party hats, Cheng begins turning his into a horn. Valerie places her hat on top of her head and dramatically strikes a pose, saying in a sultry voice, "Don't I look be:yoo:ti:ful?" Keith pops the elastic band, exclaiming, "Ow, that hurt!" Raoul and Alan tell Penny that they both want a hat decorated with the squiggly shapes, because that is a "boy hat." Penny's aunts have arrived, and they help Dilta pour punch and put candles on the cake. Next, the class sings "Happy Birthday," and Penny blows out her candles, remembering to make her birthday wish.

Penny is asked to sit in Isabel's blue chair and call children one by one to go and find a place to sit. Nancy is called first. She quickly goes directly to the "girl table" and sits at a girl spot. Her quick and determined actions indicate that it is important for her to sit at the all-girl table. Several more children are called, and they slowly find places to sit. When Laura is called she walks towards Charmaine, who is already seated. Although there is an empty seat next to Charmaine, it is a boy spot. As Laura is slowly sitting down, Nancy quickly turns around and says, "No! That's for the boys. You can't sit there." Charmaine then gets up and chooses to sit in a girl spot next to Nancy, and they both save a girl spot for Penny. Laura eventually finds a place to sit. Kim is called, but instead of finding a spot and sitting, she walks around the classroom waiting for Liza to be chosen. When Liza is picked, she and Kim walk around looking for two seats together. At this point, there are only a few seats left. Kim notices two spots next to each other and points to the dollhouse. While holding hands, they approach the dollhouse, look at the boy plates, and begin to sit down. However, Nancy notices and loudly shouts from across the room, "*No!* That's for the boys and this is a girl table." Liza and Kim get up and walk away. Here, we are able to see two conflicting views. It is apparent that Liza and Kim want to sit together more than they worry about boy plates. But Nancy does not let them overlook this.

One of Penny's aunts notices that there is not a girl place setting for Sue. She quickly exchanges the boy plate, cup, and napkin for a girl place setting. As Penny continues to call children, she reminds the girls to "sit in a girl spot, okay?" It is important to Penny that the girls get it "right."

Cheng is finally called, and he quickly runs to claim one of the few remaining boy seats. While pointing at the chair, he states, "Boy . . . I'm a boy . . . I'm here, okay?" James hesitantly heads for the "girl table," looking a bit worried when he sees one of the few empty chairs left, which is a girl spot next to Amy. Nancy quickly intervenes as she redirects him to the dollhouse, stating, "That's boys, this is a girl table." James glances around the classroom with uncertainty. Although James desires to sit in the girl spot, his choice is quickly denied by Nancy. He walks up to Isabel asking if he can sit with the girls. She tells him that he can sit anywhere that he wants. James walks back to the girls' table, looks at the paper plates, and glances toward Isabel with a confused look on his face. Although James finally sits down at the girl spot, he looks uncomfortable. Quickly one of Penny's aunts gives him the correct place setting.

Kelly and Madison are holding hands and wander around the tables, trying to figure out where they will sit. Liam and Theresa are struggling to find a "correct" place setting. Theresa notices a boy plate, points to it, and tells Liam, "You can sit here, it's a boy's." At this point, Theresa is the only student not seated, and she is still looking for a place to sit. She notices that the only available seat is across from Alan, in a boy spot, and at the all-boy table. She slowly begins to approach the table and hesitantly looks around the room. While walking toward Alan, the following transpires:

Alan: (In a loud voice, moving his hands back and forth and shaking his head) **No! Only boys at this table.**

Theresa: (Slowly sits in the chair and looks around the room)

Alan: (Places both hands on the table, gets up out of his seat, and leans forward toward Theresa's face.) This is a boy spot. Are you a b:o:y?

Theresa: (Shrugging and holding both hands out) There aren't any more spots.

Alan: **S:oo:oo**, are you a boy, Theresa?

Theresa: No. (Turns and looks away)

This exchange between Theresa and Alan shows the power of gender performances. If gender is only a performance, rather than based on biological determinism, then Theresa is in danger of being a boy, even if only for a little while. Although this might be a powerful discourse for some children, such as Madison, Theresa is not interested.

Contesting Gender Meanings With Children

After everyone is seated, the class reads a poem out loud, thanking Penny and her family for bringing all of the birthday treats. Children begin talking and appear to be having an enjoyable time with each other. I have chosen to sit with Theresa and Alan at the dollhouse. Isabel approaches one of the mixed tables and asks, "It's interesting to me where you guys chose to sit." No one responds to her comment. Nancy leans over to Penny, whispering into her ear. She then points toward Theresa, and they both begin laughing. Theresa sits quietly. Throughout the birthday party, Nancy has been powerfully regulating the gender discourse of the classroom. The moment in which Nancy leans over toward Penny is significant because it implies that Penny has gained power not just from the birthday party but from the gendered birthday party.

Isabel is serving the adults pieces of cake, purposely using the boy plates. She asks Anne to serve Dilta. Anne looks at the boy paper plate, hesitates, and says, "But . . ." Isabel tells her again to take the piece of cake to Dilta. When Dilta thanks Anne for the piece of cake, Anne looks surprised as she says, "But it's a boy plate."

As I walk past the large girl table to throw my boy plate away, Penny places her hand out to stop me.

Penny: Look at my napkin. (Shows me her napkin) Isn't it so:oo:oo pretty? I love it so much (placing it next to her heart, hugging it, and twisting back and forth)

Mindy: Really? Why?

Penny: Because she's so pretty. Hey (pointing to my plate), you have a boy plate.

Mindy: Why is it a boy plate? I don't understand.

Penny: See (pointing), two boys, truck, car.

Mindy: But I like trucks.

Penny: (Turns around and walks away)

Penny's birthday celebration is an example of how adults are attempting to contest gender meanings with children. However, in doing so, these interventions might not be empowering for all of the children. For example, how did Theresa feel because she did not end up with a girl plate?

Although the class was observed responding to the gendered place settings as they arrived in the classroom, I am still not certain how or if Isabel's intervention challenged or disrupted gender norms. Penny's birthday party allows us to see that children do know about particular gender rules, and that some children, in this case Penny and Nancy, are able to take an active part regulating them. Nancy's successful attempts at this caused me to wonder what might have happened if she had been absent. Would Laura, Liza, Kim, and James have made different choices of where they sat? On the other hand, would another student have taken on this role? When Isabel attempts to explore further with the class about their choices, she is ignored. Again, children are using silence in powerful ways. They are telling Isabel that she is getting the gender stuff wrong and, like Cheng, is considered incompetent and powerless. While I do believe that teachers should consider how their pedagogical decisions might not empower all students, I am not certain that this is a valid reason to abandon provoking children about gender discourses.

Blending In

Lunch immediately followed Penny's birthday celebration, which provided an opportunity for Isabel and me to discuss how the class responded to these deliberate gender interventions.

Isabel: I think it's interesting how they made the choices they made.

Mindy: Oh, it was. I wish I would have videotaped this. It would have been a great opportunity to see why focusing on the differences and always labeling us as boys and girls often limits our possibilities as human beings. You wouldn't believe it, Theresa nearly got stuck with a boy's plate. She walks over there and she's about to sit and Alan says, "No, no, you can't sit there, you're not a boy!"

Isabel: He thought he was safe, he thought he would be absolutely sitting next to a boy, because he had chosen that spot.

Mindy: Yeah, I don't think Alan thought about girls choosing to bend the rules. He really had a hard time with Theresa sitting there. After Theresa said there were no other places, he said, "Well, don't you know you're not a boy?" Theresa then said, "Yeah, but there aren't any other spots." So Theresa sits and then the entire all-girl table was actually regulating this. Two other groups of girls wanted to sit there; Liza and Kim wanted to.

Isabel: Well, they also wanted to be exclusive.

Mindy: That's right, and the all-girl table said, "**No,** you can't sit there, it's for boys only."

Isabel: And it was still empty at that time.

Mindy: Yes, and then Madison and Kelly went over there as well, ready to sit. They even had their hands on the seats, and it was Nancy who was regulating. She told them, "No, that's a boy table." And then Nancy tapped Penny's shoulder and told her to look. They then got really quiet and she whispered something to Penny and then they both looked at Theresa and started giggling. And you should have seen Theresa's face and body language. She was slumping and very embarrassed. I also watched Anne when you handed her the boy plates with our pieces of cake on them, and she was hesitant when you told her to take the plates to us. None of the teachers had an issue with the plates.

Isabel: What I would have loved to have happened was to have Liza at that point to use her marvelous powers of argument and say, "Kim and I want to sit together and we like dump trucks." Or something like that. It's interesting to me that she caved in.

Mindy: Yes, it is interesting. Now did anyone see what happened with James? He really didn't want to sit at a boy's spot, he wanted to sit with the girls. And I think Loren told him he could sit wherever he wanted.

Isabel: Where did he end up?

Mindy: At a boy spot.

Isabel: We have eighteen girls and there were sixteen girl spots. And Penny's aunt switched two. Sue didn't want to sit in the boy spot, so I turned around and saw the aunt switching it and Theresa sat in the boy spot.

Mindy: Yeah, but not by choice.

Isabel: Sue would have had a fit.

Mindy: In Theresa's own way she stood up to Alan. He insistently told her she was not a boy.

Loren: I also think that Alan was a little hurt that no boys went over to sit with him.

Isabel: And he chose that spot knowing, certain in his heart, that only a boy would be sitting next to him.

I have included this transcription because it shows how Isabel and I were making sense of the children's responses to the gendered places that we set. This transcription also reveals how easy it was for Penny to blend in within the social context of the classroom. Even though Isabel was aware of Penny's position as an Asian American girl in the classroom and the birthday party items were brought by Penny, both Isabel and I failed to notice and talk about Penny's experiences—we missed Penny again. This shows that while Penny skillfully performs being a nice and polite girl, she is nonetheless overlooked. This is an indicator of how some forms of gender are invisible in the classroom, and how the complicated work that is done by girls such as Penny therefore goes unnoticed. If theses gender performances continue to be overlooked, then the ways that some children understand and do gender will never have a chance to be supported or challenged by teachers.

Implications for Researching and Teaching in Early Childhood Education

Like all of the children in this class, Penny's identity is created through a complex interaction between her gender, race, class, and sexuality. She has access to a range of gender discourses, including ones that contradict gender norms. Penny, however, resists those contradictory discourses because she is constrained by the heterosexual matrix. Her survival strategy is about being invisible. Teachers and researchers need to recognize that children such as Penny often have to negotiate discourses that further reinforce the constraints of emphasized femininity. It is possible that challenging Penny's beliefs about gender runs the risk of potentially diminishing Penny and her identity as an Asian American female. If this is the case, then what are we to do? Should teachers and researchers continue to ignore Penny and how she does gender in the classroom? Of course not. Teachers and researchers must create diverse methods for seeing the complexity and specificity of children of color and their experiences (MacNaughton, 2000). In the case of Penny, this means "disrupting the associations between Asianness and goodness, queerness and whiteness, queerness and abnormality, and create associations that are less prescriptive and derogatory" (Kumashiro, 1999, p. 69). As a result, teachers and researchers might begin seeing Penny through not just a gender lens but an ethnicity lens as well. Instead of just locating gender discourses in the classroom, teachers and researchers will need to locate racial, class, and sexual discourses as well. This will enable teachers to see how these discourses intersect and how children access and use them in their daily identity work. These new ways of understanding identities will enable teachers to see more clearly which gender choices are made difficult for children like Penny and which are made easy, and how children choose to accept or resist them. For researchers this implies documenting these gender decisions and then having critical conversations with children such as Penny about the complexities of their identity work.

All discourses contain some form of counterdiscourse, and Penny's identity as an Asian American girl gives her the possibility of locating discourses of race that support different ways of performing gender. However, as an Anglo-American female, I may find recognizing these counterdiscourses difficult. Thinking about Madison and her ability to create and access the counterdiscourse of the rescuing Dalmatian puppy (see Chapter 6) raises another dilemma about Penny's agency. Since Madison is Anglo, presumably the counterdiscourses she creates are located within the dominant mainstream culture of the classroom (and society), and so they will be easily recognized and supported by her classmates. Penny might be creating counterdiscourses as well, but her peers and teachers may not be able to notice them because they might be situated within a different cultural context. It is necessary for teachers and researchers to recognize how their identities might limit how they see children in the classroom. If this is the case, then as Kumashiro (1999) argues, teachers and researchers must recognize children's differences in order to understand their subjectivity. This is possible by understanding how "...children in the classroom differ in relation to gender, race, class, and sexuality and how this enables them to shape the experiences of themselves and others (MacNaughton, 2000, p. 79). The complexities of race and gender and how they play out in the classroom might begin making sense to teachers if they actively locate and identify them. Overall, Penny and the fact that her gender work is easily overlooked are important reminders to teachers and researchers about the necessity for consciously locating gender in the classroom. By first locating gender, if then becomes possible to recognize the intersections of gender, race, class, and sexuality and how children are constructing their social identities in the early childhood setting. Then, power and the part that it plays in shaping relationships will become evident. However, this will entail a different set of goals for how teachers and researchers enact their practices.

7
RETHINKING GENDER AND
EARLY CHILDHOOD TEACHING

As this study has shown, it is clear that young children take an active part in the social construction of gender. Not only do children understand gender discourses, but they are also capable of accessing them in order to regulate gender in their everyday lives. Young children and the gender discourses they take part in are not determined exclusively by biological factors, nor are they only a consequence of being socialized into particular ways of being; rather, they are the result of how the children make sense of and enact gender discourses every day. They use these gender discourses to construct themselves as girls or boys, or in the case of Madison something in between. The children collectively draw on the knowledge of their culture that they understand as supporting the types of play they desire. In this case, it is their play that makes them feel good, powerful, and desirable to others.

Pulling It All Together

Feminist poststructuralism and queer theory have opened up new ways for listening to, observing, and interpreting children's talk and actions in the classroom. Such postdevelopmental perspectives can assist us to conceptualize gender as a social, historical, cultural, and political construction, and to recognize that young children take an active part in their gender construction. As the classroom examples of children's play have shown, the dominant discourse is about wanting to "play it straight." Both Alan and Penny take up these discourses daily, while Madison attempts to find other, and for her, more liberating discourses to engage with.

We saw in Chapter 3 how five gender discourses (wearing femininity, body movements, makeup, beauty, and fashion talk) work in the early childhood classroom and how they constitute an integral part of the heterosexual matrix. However, it is not enough for teachers simply to notice and recognize these gender discourses in the classroom. If we are serious about disrupting gender norms, then we as teachers must step out of our safety zones and actively respond to the gender discourses that children are drawing from when they are in the classroom and help them to challenge these taken-for-granted norms. Moving away from a single way of knowing, in this case developmentalism, makes room for multiple perspectives, which in turn influence innovative kinds of teaching decisions and practices. As children's talk and actions take on new meanings, so will teaching. Rethinking teaching strategies and envisioning new kinds of classrooms will be hard, because this is about trying to create a space that we often cannot see ourselves.

Queer Possibilities

I believe that the ways in which Isabel addresses gender in her classroom offer a starting point for teachers to challenge gender norms. However, I think that teachers can and need to push the pedagogical and theoretical boundaries even more if we intend seriously to rethink gender and teaching in the early childhood classroom. New pedagogies, or rather postdevelopmental pedagogies, are needed in order to create early childhood classrooms as places where children who want or need to transgress gender boundaries can do so.

Queer theory provides a framework for rethinking pedagogies aimed at promoting equity and social justice. First, queer theory does not mean teaching about sex or same-sex sexuality. Instead, it provides an alternative perspective that is helpful for challenging generally accepted notions of gender, specifically for recognizing how heterosexual discourses dominate in the classroom and how they play an integral part in creating what children consider to be normal and right behaviors. Most importantly, teaching queerly is about exploring and then disrupting assumptions about diversity, identities, teaching, learning, and young children (Sears, 1999).

I do not believe that there are easy answers when seeking to reconceptualize gender and early childhood teaching. Isabel used effective techniques, such as highlighting gender resistance and drawing attention to gender practices, as a beginning to disrupting this process. Sears (1999) also suggests three ways forward for teachers seeking to queer their classrooms. He suggests that teachers working from a queer perspective must create classrooms that *challenge categorical thinking, promote interpersonal intelligence,* and *foster critical consciousness.*

So far, this book has drawn primarily from feminist poststructuralism and queer theory to interpret gender in the classroom. Now I would like to take these postdevelopmental perspectives and push them further, using them for imagining queer possibilities in the early childhood classroom.

Creating Classrooms That Challenge Categorical Thinking

The children in Isabel's classroom were observed challenging categorical thinking about gender. Davies (2003) supports this idea, as she believes that the only way that gender norms can be subverted is by children taking part in different kinds of gender discourses. This implies that teachers must ensure that multiple gender discourses are available for children to access. Madison had the confidence to create and engage in counterdiscourses. However, Cheng wanted to be a boy differently, and play with "girly" things, but the children regulated his desires, and he learned that this was not acceptable behavior for boys in this classroom.

This classroom community allowed and supported critical conversations about gender to occur and in doing so provided glimpses of possibilities of change. Although these discussions happened between individual children, they also happened within the context of certain classroom structures that Isabel created, such as work share and show-and-tell. Both of these classroom routines provided opportunities for Isabel to find out what children knew about gender, and then to challenge the ways that some children thought about gender differences. An example of this was seen during show-and-tell, as children shared the lunch boxes they brought to school. A classroom discussion transpired that included Madison and Katy challenging some of Alan's rigid beliefs about boys and girls. Alan's categorical thinking could have been challenged further by asking him directly why he believed that boys don't play with Barbies.

Another way that categorical thinking can be challenged in the classroom is being conscious of the language and actions that we enact. Having a girls' line and a boys' line only reinforces gender differences, especially when the school community (i.e., other teachers, children, and parents) sees and hears the girls' line as quiet and the boys' line as loud and rambunctious. Therefore, instead of having lines based on gender differences, teachers can disrupt this dichotomy by having children choose partners when lining up, or not lining up at all.

Categorical thinking can also be challenged by attempting to restructure power relations between children in a range of social contexts. Gender work should not just happen exclusively in learning centers that are thought of as primarily "boy" or "girl" centers, because gender is socially constructed everywhere. Instead, teachers must recognize that children are constantly involved in discursive practices and that the social contexts of the classroom will influence power relationships and subjectivity in different ways. Additionally, it is imperative for teachers to realize that children's subjectivities and relationships occur within the confines of *heterosexualized* classrooms.

Creating Classrooms That Promote Interpersonal Intelligence

Within a poststructuralist framework, interpersonal intelligence is just a way of saying that a person is confident in negotiating a variety of discourses. I believe that Madison has this skill. For example, when Madison was observed trying to play with Alan and Keith in the dramatic play area, she decided not to try to change their minds. Instead, she seemed to know that even if she did play with them, it would not be an enjoyable experience because of the way in which Alan was trying to wield power.

Madison is confident about her female identities and is able to create alternative ways of being within these, such as pretending to be a teenage boy or a male dog. Being a dog allows Madison to be adventurous (rescuing others) as well as loveable, and all without having to play the human heterosexual game.

Madison shows her gender competence in getting more girls to give Lego a try. What is important here is that the girls might have read this strategy differently if it was Isabel suggesting that more girls go and play with Lego. Coming from a peer, Madison, who seems so secure about her gender choices, made playing at Lego a real possibility for some of the girls. How does this kind of student-led activism happen? It happens because Madison has the skills to make her gender choices seem both reasonable and desirable. Teachers will need to recognize how children such as Madison are subverting the dominant discourse, and draw attention to this work in supportive ways. Noticing the gender work that children are doing and bringing this work to the center of the curriculum sends a message to all children about the importance of this work. Yet a feminist poststructuralist perspective believes that children do have agency, and therefore not everyone will simply accept a teacher's interventions. On the other hand, it also means that it is possible for children to challenge the normative ways that gender is understood and practiced.

Creating Classrooms That Foster Critical Consciousness

Creating classrooms that foster critical consciousness will not happen overnight. Instead, it requires strategic planning on the part of teachers. The multiple discourses and subjectivities that we are currently involved in allow girls and boys to take up and embody a range of ways of being. My hope for the future is that multiple ways of being gendered will be acceptable, instead of relying on the heterosexual matrix to regulate how girls and boys should be in relationship to each other and within the world.

Becoming critical and conscious of the relationships we have with children is one step toward creating a classroom that fosters a critical consciousness about gender. Instead of assuming that the relationships we have with students are objective and gender-neutral, it is vital to recognize that gendered power relationships do exist and how gender discourses influence these relationships. Revisiting the examples presented in Chapter 4 clearly shows how both Loren and I were a part of a gendered power relationship with Alan. Queer theory pushes the analysis of the teacher–student relationship by locating the *heterosexualized* relationship that existed between two female adults and a male student. Although I became conscious of this gendered power relationship, and the ways in which gender discourses were marginalizing and silencing me as a female, I failed to intervene. At the time, I could not imagine that I was a part of the heterosexual matrix, and I did not have the strategies needed to challenge this gender discourse. When teachers realize that they are a part of gendered power relationships, then it becomes possible to take action. This will happen in part by directly talking to children about when a teacher feels uncomfortable or marginalized and why.

A critical consciousness about gender inequity was supported when Isabel exposed Madison's Lego concerns to the entire class, discussing these Lego issues with the class during work share and enlarging the audience by extending the conversation to include their third-grade story partners. In doing so, the older students shared their own experiences about gender norms and inequities found with Lego action figures and other highly gendered toys and computer games. Madison's Lego concerns also appeared in the Memory Web as "The Lego people answered Madison's letter. And they sent us Lego girls." As explained earlier, the Memory Web is generated by students, rather than Isabel. This shows how Madison's classmates are aware of her gender work and how the Memory Web shares with families what is going on in the classroom.

Another way that critical consciousness can be promoted is by assisting children to realize that they are involved in discursive practices and to see how they are choosing to locate themselves within these discourses. This will help children make sense of why particular discourses are more desirable than others, and why they make the choices that they do. By having the freedom to position themselves in multiple ways, children have the opportunity to experience a range of discourses, providing them "access to imaginary worlds in which new metaphors, new forms of social relations, and new patterns of power and desire are explored" (Davies, 2003, p. 167). Not only does this promote a critical consciousness about gender, but it also attempts to disrupt categorical thinking.

Supporting Risky Gender Work in the Classroom

If teachers believe that there are several ways to be gendered, then it is necessary to create strategies to support the risky gender work that all children bravely do in the classroom. However, it is not just children who will need support; teachers who challenge the dominant discourses in early childhood will too. Although a growing number of teachers are beginning to challenge and subvert the dominant discourses in early childhood, including teachers who are challenging gender in their practice by drawing from postdevelopmental theories (Blaise & Andrew, 2005; Boldt, 1997; Campbell & Smith, 2001; MacNaughton, 2000), this is risky teaching. Bryson & de Castell (1997) write about their experiences of creating a queer praxis as being not only risky teaching, but also as agonizing and difficult.

In conclusion, postdevelopmentalism has dramatically influenced my life and work as a female researcher and teacher. I have become aware of the complexities and politics of gender, teaching, and researching, and how I am discursively constructed within my personal and professional relationships. As Bryson & de Castell (1997) write about their own experiences with risky teaching, I too have had difficult times doing this kind of work. The questions that have been raised throughout my study have not always been easy or comfortable ones. They have pushed me into rethinking my own hopes and desires for using alternative theoretical frameworks, like feminist poststructuralism and queer theory, to generate new knowledge in the field of early childhood education. These new ways of seeing teaching, learning, gender, and young children can seem too radical or outrageous for some teachers. However, I believe that drawing from multiple perspectives is necessary for challenging and transgressing gender inequities and ultimately improving the lives of girls, women, boys, and men.

APPENDIX

Symbols Used in the Presentation of Transcripts

Symbol	Meaning
Bold	Indicates words heavily emphasized by the speaker
? , !	Used to indicate that an utterance was a question or an exclamation
//	Indicates an interruption
. . .	Indicates a pause, with the number of dots indicating the length of the pause
do::n't	Indicate a prolonged sound; the greater the number of colons, the more prolonged the sound
quiet	Marks talk that has a noticeably lower or higher volume than the surrounding talk
{ }	Indicates indecipherable comments
( )	Statements in parentheses describe the context of an utterance and any other information recorded in the field notes
___	Indicates that words overlap or are uttered simultaneously
.	Indicates the deletion of data in a transcript
.	
.	

These transcription symbols were adapted from Danby (1998).

REFERENCES

AAUW (American Association of University Women) (1992). *How schools shortchange girls: A study of major findings on girls and education.* Washington, DC: American Association of University Women Educational Foundation.

Alldred, P. (1998). Ethnography and discourse analysis: Dilemmas in representing the voices of children. In J. Ribbens & R. Edwards (Eds.), *Feminist dilemmas in qualitative research: Public knowledge and private lives* (pp. 147–170). Thousand Oaks, CA: Sage Publications.

Alloway, N. (1995). *The construction of gender in early childhood.* Victoria, Australia: Dolphin Press.

Almy, M., & Genishi, C. (1979). *Ways of studying children.* New York: Teachers College Press.

Bandura, A. (1977). *Social learning theory.* Englewood Cliffs, NJ: Prentice-Hall.

Bandura, A., & Walters, R. H. (1963). *Social learning and personality development.* New York: Holt, Rinehart & Winston.

Basow, S. (1986). *Gender stereotypes: Traditions and alternatives.* Monterey, CA: Brooks/Cole.

Berger, P. (1976). *Sociology: A biographical approach.* NY: Penguin.

Blaise, M. & Andrew, Y. (2005) How "bad" can it be?: Troubling gender, sexuality, and teaching in early childhood education. In N. Yelland (Ed.), *Critical issues in early childhood* (pp. 49–57). Berkshire, England: McGraw-Hill/Open University Press.

Bohan, J. S. (1997). Regarding gender: Essentialism, constructionism, and feminist psychology. In M. M. Gergen & S. N. Davis (Eds.), *Toward a new psychology of gender: A reader* (pp. 31–47). New York: Routledge.

Boldt, G. (1997). Sexist and heterosexist responses to gender bending. In J. Tobin (Ed.), *Making a place for pleasure in early childhood education* (pp. 188–213). New Haven, CT: Yale University Press.

Boomer, G. (1992). Literacy: The epic challenge beyond progressivism. Address to the Joint Australian Reading Association and Australian Association for the Teaching of English national conference, "Across the borders: Language at the interface." Darwin, Australia.

Bredekamp, S., & Copple, C. (1997). *Developmentally appropriate practice in early childhood programs serving children from birth through age 8* (Rev. ed.). Washington, DC: National Association for the Education of Young Children.

Britzman, D. (1995). Is there a queer pedagogy? Or, stop reading straight. *Educational Theory, 45*(2), 151–165.

Brophy, J., & Good, T. (1974). *Teacher-student relationships: Causes and consequences.* New York: Holt, Rinehart, & Winston.

Brown, M. (1975). *Stone soup: An old tale.* New York: Charles Scribner's Sons.

Browne, N. (2004). *Gender equity in the early years.* Berkshire, England: Open University Press.

Bryson, M., & de Castell, S. (1997). Queer pedagogy?!: Praxis makes im/perfect. In S. de Castell & M. Bryson (Eds.), *Radical In<ter>ventions: Identity, politics, and difference/s in educational praxis* (pp. 269–293). Albany: State University of New York Press.

Burman, E. (1992). Feminism and discourse in developmental psychology: Power, subjectivity, and interpretation. *Feminism & Psychology, 2*(1), 45–60.

Butler, J. (1990). *Gender trouble: Feminisms and the subversion of identity.* New York: Routledge.

Campbell, S. & Smith, K. (2001). Equity observations and images of fairness in childhood. In S. Grieshaber & G.S. Cannella (Eds.), *Embracing identities in early childhood education: Diversity and possibilities* (pp. 89–102). New York: Teachers College Press.

Connell, R. W. (1987). *Gender and power.* Stanford, CA: Stanford University Press.

Connell, R. W. (1995). *Masculinities.* Berkeley: University of California Press.

Connell, R. W. (1996). Teaching the boys: New research on masculinity and gender strategies for schools. *Teachers College Record, 98*(2), 206–235.

Connolly, P. (1998). *Racism, gender identities, and young children.* New York: Routledge.

Cook, J. A., & Fonow, M. M. (1990). Knowledge and women's interests: Issues of epistemology and methodology in feminist sociological research. In J. M. Nielson (Ed.), *Feminist research methods: Exemplary readings in the social sciences* (pp. 69–93). San Francisco: Westview Press.

Danby, S. (1998). The serious and playful work of gender: Talk and social order in a preschool classroom. In N. Yelland (Ed.), *Gender in early childhood* (pp. 175–205). New York: Routledge.

Davies, B. (1994). *Poststructuralist theory and classroom practice.* Victoria, Australia: Deakin University Press.

Davies, B. (2003). *Frogs and snails and feminist tales: Preschool children and gender* (Rev. ed.). Sydney, Australia: Allen & Unwin.

Davies, B. (2004). Introduction: Poststructuralist lines of flight in Australia. *International Journal of Qualitative Studies in Education, 17*(1), 3–9.

Derman-Sparks, L. (1991). *Anti-bias curriculum: Tools for empowering young children.* Washington, DC: National Association for the Education of Young Children.

Donovan, J. (1992). *Feminist theory: The intellectual traditions of American feminism.* New York: Continuum.

Ebbeck, M. (1984). Equity for boys and girls: Some important issues. *Early Child Development and Care, 18,* 119–131.

Fausto-Sterling, A. (1992). *Myths of gender: Biological theories about women and men* (2nd ed.). New York: Basic Books.

Fay, B. (1987). *Critical social science.* Ithaca, NY: Cornell University Press.

Fine, M. (1994). Dis-stance and other stances: Negotiations of power inside feminist research. In A. Gitlin (Ed.), *Power and method: Political activism and educational research* (pp. 13–35). New York: Routledge.

Flax, J. (1990). Postmodernism and gender relations in feminist theory. In L.J. Nicholson (Ed.), *Feminism/postmodernism* (pp. 39–62). New York: Routledge.

Foucault, M. (1972). *The archaeology of knowledge and the discourse on language* (A. M. Sheridan Smith, Trans.). New York: Pantheon Books.

Foucault, M. (1980a). Truth and power. In C. Gordon (Ed.), *Power/knowledge: Selected interviews and other writings, 1972–1977* (pp. 111–133). New York: Pantheon Books.

Foucault, M. (1980b). Two lectures. In C. Gordon (Ed.), *Power/knowledge: Selected interviews and other writings, 1972–1977* (pp. 78–108). New York: Pantheon Books.

Freire, P. (1994). *Pedagogy of the oppressed* (new revised 20th Anniversary ed). New York: Continuum.

Gallas, K. (1994). *The languages of learning: How children talk, write, dance, draw and sing their understanding of the world.* New York: Teachers College Press.

Gallas, K. (1998). *"Sometimes I can be anything": Power, gender, and identity in a primary classroom.* New York: Teachers College Press.

Gavey, N. (1997). Feminist poststructuralism and discourse analysis. In M. M. Gergen and S. N. Davis (Eds.), *Toward a new psychology of gender: A reader* (pp. 49–64). New York: Routledge.

Gill, R. (1995). Relativism, reflexivity, and politics: Interrogating discourse analysis from a feminist perspective. In S. Wilkinson & C. Kitzinger (Eds.), *Feminism and discourse: Psychological perspectives* (pp. 165–186). Thousand Oaks, CA: Sage.

Gitlin, A., & Russell, R. (1994). Alternative methodologies and the research context. In A. Gitlin (Ed.), *Power and method: political activism and educational research* (pp. 181–202). New York: Routledge.

Glesne, C., & Peshkin, A. (1992). *Becoming qualitative researchers: An introduction.* White Plains, NY: Longman.

Gramsci, A. (1971). *Selections from the prison notebooks.* London: Lawrence and Wishart.

Grieshaber, S., & Cannella, G. S. (Eds.) (2001). *Embracing identities in early childhood education: Diversity and possibilities.* New York: Teachers College Press.

Hauser, M., & Jipson, J. (1997). *Intersections: Feminisms/early childhoods.* New York: Peter Lang.

Hargreaves, D. H. (1967). *Social relations in a secondary school.* London: Routledge.

Henriques, J., Hollway, W., Urwin, C., Venn, C., & Walkerdine, V. (Eds.) (1984). *Changing the subject: Psychology, social regulation, and subjectivity.* London: Methuen.

Hicks, D. (1995–96). Discourse, learning, and teaching. *Review of Research in Education, 21,* 49–93.

Hollway, W. (1984). Gender difference and the production of subjectivity. In J. Henriques, W. Hollway, C. Urwin, C. Venn, & V. Walkerdine (Eds.), *Changing the subject: Psychology, social regulation, and subjectivity* (pp. 227–263). London: Methuen.

Howes, C. (1992). *The collaborative construction of pretend.* Albany, Stanford University Press.

Irigaray, L. (1981). The sex which is not one. In E. Marks & I. de Courtivorn (Eds.), *New French feminisms* (pp. 99–106). Brighton, England: Harvester.

Jayaratne, T. E., & Stewart, A. J. (1995). Quantitative and qualitative methods in the social sciences: Feminist issues and practical strategies. In J. Holland & M. Blair (Eds.), *Debates and issues in feminist research and pedagogy* (pp. 217–234). Philadelphia: Open University Press.

Jones, M. (1989). Gender bias in classroom interactions. *Contemporary Education, 60,* 216–222.

Katz, L. G. (1996). Child development knowledge and teacher preparation: Confronting assumptions. *Early Childhood Research Quarterly, 11,* 135–146.

Kessler, S., & Swadener, B. (1992). *Reconceptualizing the early childhood curriculum: Beginning the dialogue.* New York: Teachers College Press.

Kimmel, M. (1990). After fifteen years: The impact of the sociology of masculinity on the masculinity of sociology. In J. Heam & D. Morgan (Eds.), *Men, masculinities and social theory.* London: Unwin Hyman.

Klein, V. (1946). *The feminine character.* London: Routledge.

Kumashiro, K. K. (1999). Reading queer Asian American masculinities. In W. J. Letts & J. T. Sears (Eds.), *Queering elementary education: Advancing the dialogue about sexualities and schooling* (pp. 61–70). Lanham, MD: Rowman & Littlefield.

Lather, P. (1991). *Getting smart: Feminist research and pedagogy with/in the postmodern.* New York: Routledge.

Lather, P. (1992). Critical frames in educational research: Feminist and poststructural perspectives. *Theory into Practice, 31*(2), 87–99.

Lather, P. (1995). Feminist perspectives on empowering research methodologies. In J. Holland & M. Blair (Eds.), *Debates and issues in feminist research and pedagogy* (pp. 292–307). Philadelphia, The Open University Press.

Lee, S. J. (1996). *Unraveling the "model minority" stereotype: Listening to Asian American youth.* New York: Teachers College Press.

Lindsey, L. L. (1990). *Gender roles: A sociological perspective.* Princeton, NJ: Prentice-Hall.

Lockheed, M. (1984). *Final report: A study of sex equity in classroom interactions.* Washington, DC: National Institute of Education.

Lorber, J. (1994). *Paradoxes of gender.* New York: Vail-Ballou Press.

Lubeck, S. (1996). Deconstructing "child development knowledge" and "teacher preparation." *Early Childhood Research Quarterly, 11,* 147–167.

Luke, A. (1995). Text and discourse in education: An introduction to critical discourse analysis. *Review of Research in Education, 21,* 3–48.

Lynn, D. B. (1969). *Parental and sex role identification: A theoretical formulation.* Berkeley, CA: McCutchan.

MacNaughton, G. (1994). "You can be dad": Gender and power in domestic discourse and fantasy play within early childhood. *Journal for Australian Research in Early Childhood Education, 1,* 93–102.

MacNaughton, G. (1996). Is Barbie to blame? Reconsidering how children learn gender. *Australian Journal of Early Childhood, 21*(4), 18–24.

MacNaughton, G. (1997). Who's got the power? Rethinking gender equity strategies in early childhood. *International Journal of Early Years Education, 5*(1), 57–66.

MacNaughton, G. (1998). Improving our gender equity "tools": A case for discourse analysis. In N. Yelland (Ed.), *Gender in early childhood* (pp. 149–174). New York: Routledge.

MacNaughton, G. (2000). *Rethinking gender in early childhood education.* London: Paul Chapman.

Mallory, B. L., & New, R. S. (1994). *Diversity and developmentally appropriate practices: Challenges for early childhood education.* New York: Teachers College Press.

Measor, L., & Sikes, P. J. (1992). *Gender and schools.* New York: Cassell.

Mischel, W. (1966). A social learning view of sex differences in behavior. In E. E. Maccoby (Ed.), *The development of sex differences* (pp. 56–81). Stanford, CA: Stanford University Press.

Nicholson, L. (1994). Interpreting gender. *Signs, 20*(1), 79–105.

Nielson, J. M. (1990). Introduction. In J. M. Nielson (Ed.), *Feminist research methods: Exemplary readings in the social sciences* (pp. 1–34). San Francisco: Westview Press.

Oakley, A. (1972). *Sex, gender, and society.* New York: Harper and Row.

Paechter, C. F. (1998). *Educating the other: Gender, power and schooling.* Washington, DC: Falmer Press.

Parten, M. B. (1932). Social participation among pre-school children. *Journal of Abnormal and Social Psychology, 27,* 243–269.

Patton, M. Q. (1990). *Qualitative evaluation and research methods.* Newbury Park, CA: Sage Publications.

Phelan, S. (Ed.) (1997). *Playing with fire: Queer politics, queer theories.* New York: Routledge.

Ribbens, J., & Edwards, R. (1998). *Feminist dilemmas in qualitative research: Public knowledge and private lives.* Thousand Oaks, CA: Sage.

Rich, A. (1980). Compulsory heterosexuality and the lesbian existence. *Signs: Journal of Women in Culture and Society, 5,* 631–660.

Roberts, H. (1981). *Doing feminist research.* Boston: Routledge and Kegan Paul.

Roman, L., & Apple, M. (1990). Is naturalism a move away from positivism? Materialist and feminist approaches to subjectivity in ethnographic research. In E. Eisner and A. Peshkin (Eds.), *Qualitative inquiry in education* (pp. 38–73). New York: Teachers College Press.

Sadker, M., & Sadker, D. (1986). Sexism in the classroom: From grade school to graduate school. *Phi Delta Kappan, 67*(7), 512–515.

Sadker, M., & Sadker, D. (1995). *Failing at fairness: How our schools cheat girls.* New York: Simon & Schuster.

Sears, J. T. (1999). Teaching queerly: Some elementary propositions. In W. J. Letts & J. T. Sears (Eds.), *Queering elementary education: Advancing the dialogue about sexualities and schooling* (pp. 3–14). Lanham, MD: Rowman & Littlefield.

Sedgwick, E. K. (1990). *Epistemology of the closet.* Berkeley: University of California Press.

Silin, J. (1995). *Sex, death, and the education of young children: Our passion for ignorance in the age of AIDS.* New York: Teachers College Press.

Stanley, L., & Wise, S. (1993). *Breaking out again: Feminist ontology and epistemology* (New ed.). New York: Routledge.

Stott, F., & Bowman, B. (1996). Child development knowledge: A slippery base for practice. *Early Childhood Research Quarterly, 11,* 169–183.

Thorne, B. (1995). *Gender play: Girls and boys in school.* New Brunswick, NJ: Rutgers University Press.

Tobin, J. (1995). Poststructural research in early childhood education. In J. A. Hatch (Ed.), *Qualitative research in early childhood settings* (pp. 223–243). Westport, CT: Praeger.

Tobin, J. (Ed.) (1997). *Making a place for pleasure in early childhood education.* New Haven, CT: Yale University Press.

Vygotsky, L. (1986). *Thought and language.* Cambridge, MA: MIT Press.

Walkerdine, V. (1986). Poststructuralist theory and everyday social practices: The family and the school. In S. Wilkinson (Ed.), *Feminist social psychology: Developing theory and practice* (pp. 57–76). Philadelphia: Open University Press.

Walkerdine, V. (1990). *Schoolgirl fictions.* London: Verso.

Warner, M. (Ed.) (1993). *Fear of a queer planet: Queer politics and social theory.* Minneapolis: University of Minnesota Press.

Weedon, C. (1997). *Feminist practice and poststructuralist theory.* Oxford, England: Blackwell.

Weiner, G. (1994). *Feminisms in education: An introduction.* Philadelphia: Open University Press.

Wilkinson, S. (1986). *Feminist social psychology: Developing theory and practice.* Philadelphia: Open University Press.

Willis, P. (1977). *Learning to labour: How working class kids get working class jobs.* Farnborough England: Saxon House.

Yelland, N. (1998). *Gender in early childhood.* New York: Routledge.

Yelland, N. (2005). *Critical issues in early childhood education.* Soffolka, England: McGraw-Hill/Open University Press.

INDEX